CHANGING COURSE

CHANGING COURSE

Inspiration, Ideas and Insights for Starting Again from the CEO Who Became a Caddie

NEIL FRANCIS

HAY HOUSE

Carlsbad, California • New York City • London • Sydney
Johannesburg • Vancouver • Hong Kong • New Delhi

First published and distributed in the United Kingdom by:
Hay House UK Ltd, Astley House, 33 Notting Hill Gate, London W11 3JQ
Tel: +44 (0)20 3675 2450; Fax: +44 (0)20 3675 2451
www.hayhouse.co.uk

Published and distributed in the United States of America by:
Hay House Inc., PO Box 5100, Carlsbad, CA 92018-5100
Tel: (1) 760 431 7695 or (800) 654 5126
Fax: (1) 760 431 6948 or (800) 650 5115
www.hayhouse.com

Published and distributed in Australia by:
Hay House Australia Ltd, 18/36 Ralph St, Alexandria NSW 2015
Tel: (61) 2 9669 4299; Fax: (61) 2 9669 4144
www.hayhouse.com.au

Published and distributed in the Republic of South Africa by:
Hay House SA (Pty) Ltd, PO Box 990, Witkoppen 2068
Tel/Fax: (27) 11 467 8904
www.hayhouse.co.za

Published and distributed in India by:
Hay House Publishers India, Muskaan Complex, Plot No.3, B-2,
Vasant Kunj, New Delhi 110 070
Tel: (91) 11 4176 1620; Fax: (91) 11 4176 1630
www.hayhouse.co.in

Distributed in Canada by:
Raincoast, 9050 Shaughnessy St, Vancouver BC V6P 6E5
Tel: (1) 604 323 7100; Fax: (1) 604 323 2600

A catalogue record for this book is available from the British Library.

ISBN: 978-1-78180-152-9

Printed and bound in Great Britain by TJ International, Padstow, Cornwall.

This book is dedicated to my mum and my late dad (Ed Francis, 1928–2012). In the 1960s they took the bold and brave decision to change course. They uprooted from the northeast of England to Tuscany in Italy, in order to provide a better life for their family. A great example of what this book is all about.

CONTENTS

ACKNOWLEDGEMENTS

There are many people who have helped make this book a reality, so a massive 'thank you' goes to the following:

Alastair Bruce, who worked with me to shape the book, did the initial edits and supported me in so many ways. Thanks also to his colleagues at Shaw Marketing and Design.

Gavin Cargill, Simon Duffy, Paul Francis, Helen Kibby, Howard Thain and Tim Walsh, who read the manuscript and gave me great feedback.

Andy Hamilton, the current CEO of Company Net, for all his support and help; all the staff – former and current – at Company Net and all the clients I have worked with.

Steve Dalgleish, Mark Elliott, Kevin Grainger, Simon Scott and John Shaw – and everyone else who didn't say 'no' when I contacted them and said: 'You know this book I'm writing?

Well, I was just wondering if you could help me with…'

A special thank you to Sam Fox – starter and caddie master at The North Berwick Golf Club – who gave me the opportunity to become a caddie, and supported me thereafter. And a big thank you also to his colleague, Malcolm Gibson. Also Chris Spencer, secretary at The North Berwick Golf Club. And, crucially, all the golfers I've had the pleasure of caddying for at the club, and all the caddies I work with.

Dr David Gillespie, my neuropsychologist, whose support, advice and encouragement following my stroke has made this book, and the many other new things in my life, possible.

The brilliant team at Hay House, especially Amy Kiberd and Juile Oughton. Also Michelle Pilley who took a chance on an unknown author, and my editor, Debra Wolter.

And finally, and most importantly, to my family. To my wife, Louise, for all the love, encouragement and incredible help and support she has given me over so many years. To my children, Jack, Lucy and Sam, whose great humour, patience and love have helped me in so many ways. They have all played such a key role in my recovery from the stroke.

And, finally, to my daft dog, Dougal – our long walks on the beaches of North Berwick gave me the time to think about and plan this book!

Introduction

BRAD THE STOCKBROKER

You think you have your career mapped out. You think your children will need you forever. You've recently had a health check and everything seemed to be okay. You might be a CEO, a housewife, a marketing manager, an entrepreneur or a lawyer.

Life is fine. And then it kicks you in the teeth.

You're told that you're going to be made redundant from your job after 20 years' service. Or, on a Sunday evening, the idea of going to work the next morning fills you with dread. You've come to the realization that your current job is not what you *really* want to do. You feel trapped.

Perhaps your son or daughter is about to leave home for university. Things are changing, and you have no idea what you're going to do with your time from now on.

Maybe you dream of doing something completely different with your life, but you don't actually know *how* to go about it. Or perhaps you've had a serious health scare and, although you are now recovering, it still means that you won't be able to do the job or role you did before.

You have to start again, and change the course of your life.

But how would you do that?

When events like this occur, it's easy to see them in a negative light. In fact, many people can become confused, frightened or depressed. But, believe me, there is some positive news. In fact, I would say *excellent* news. And I'm going to share it with you in this book.

You see, I was in one of these scenarios – that last one about the health scare. A few years ago (in October 2006), at the age of 41, I had a stroke. Quite a serious one. The doctors told me it had been caused by a blood clot in my leg (a deep vein thrombosis, or DVT) that I'd developed during a flight to Boston in the USA on business.

The timing of the stroke was far from ideal (but when is it ever?) It happened when I was on holiday with my family on Arran, a small island off the west coast of Scotland. One moment I was getting out of my car, the next I couldn't speak, I couldn't see out of one eye and I thought I was going to fall down. I felt incredibly weird.

I was transferred from the island to a larger hospital on the mainland. There, the doctors quickly told me that I'd suffered a stroke. The medical term for the type of stroke I'd had is a 'paradoxical embolism', and, ironically, the speech and cognitive impairments it left me with makes it very difficult for me to say or spell that!

So I just say that I had a stroke.

After a while, I was moved on to a hospital in Edinburgh, Scotland's capital city, to be closer to my family, and later I was allowed to return home. Then followed regular visits to my doctor, new medications, appointments with a speech therapist, and the many (and ongoing) sessions with my brilliant neuropsychologist. I had numerous medical scans, tests and assessments – all courtesy of the UK's fantastic National Health Service!

For about a year after the stroke, I couldn't really communicate. Words that were in my mind just wouldn't come out, even though I knew what I wanted to say. For example, in the early days, I would sit with my speech therapist and she'd ask me to describe a scene from a children's picture book: on the beach, say, or at the park. I really struggled to *say* what I was seeing. I knew in my *mind* that it was a ball the boy was kicking, or that it was a dog running next to the girl, but I just couldn't *say* it.

It was incredibly frustrating. And if I did eventually get the words out, they were often wrong and sometimes highly inappropriate – just ask my kids!

Also, for a while, my memory was non-existent. I couldn't even remember the names of my children. The small memories – like passwords – had gone, as well as the big ones – like important family events. It felt as if I was constantly living in the 'now' – with no sense of time. In my mind, something that had occurred an hour previously could have happened a year ago, or vice versa!

I felt very confused and highly charged emotionally. I would burst into tears unexpectedly, and at the most inappropriate times! My mood would go up and down, and I was incredibly tired. I had difficulty expressing my thoughts, feelings and emotions clearly. And trying to focus on more than one thing at a time was just impossible. I was unable to read or write, and was forced to stop driving temporarily.

Gone in an instant

All of these things are not particularly good attributes if – as I was – you happen to be the CEO of a highly successful internet and web development company.

Eleven years previously, in 1996, I'd co-founded a business called Company Net. At that time, the worldwide web – and all its potential – was in its infancy in the UK. Over the next few years, I worked with some of the biggest global brands – including Disney, BP, Microsoft and Coca-Cola – on projects across the world.

Company Net built fantastic and complex websites for some of the planet's largest companies, and I travelled the world: leading projects, winning awards, attending conferences and speaking at events.

I led Company Net to a point where it was bought by one of our major clients, and then, two years later, I organized a team to help me buy it back! I employed many highly skilled people, was my own boss and headed a great leadership team. I was incredibly proud of the business and everything about it.

I loved it all. But the stroke blew all that away. One day I was a CEO, and the next… well, some bloke who used to run an internet company. My identity, my role, my status and my purpose had gone.

I could no longer do my job as CEO. I had to stop attending meetings. The pitches I'd once made were now done by other people in the business. My trips to the USA, Africa and Europe came to an abrupt halt. The corporate event invitations were now sent to other employees, and the clients I once lunched with met with the new CEO.

It took me a while to figure it out (remember, parts of my brain were out of action), but actually, I was going to have to completely change tack. I was beginning the process of starting again and changing the course of my life.

Where that would lead, I had no idea. All I knew was this: I could no longer manage the job I was passionate about and loved doing. It was like being 18 again and wondering what I should do with my life. But I was 41! With a mortgage to pay, a family to support and a wide range of responsibilities.

However, I did have a few things in my favour. I'd had the experience of being a CEO for 11 years – even though I wouldn't be one again – and I'd been on the board of several other companies and charities. I had a strong background in marketing and sales, and prior to co-founding Company Net I'd worked for one of Scotland's top marketing and design agencies.

And, fortunately, I had a bit of money to tide me over until I decided what on earth I was going to do.

Slowly, I started to realize that this situation could, potentially, be a fantastic opportunity. Yes, now I had some serious limitations, but I've always had a positive outlook on life. I simply had to *start accepting* my health situation. Nothing was going to change it – my neuropsychologist had told me that – so I just had to move forwards.

To my mind, I now had a blank canvas. I was being given a second chance to do things differently in a new career (whatever that would be), and also in my spare time and with my friends and family – in fact, in all areas of my life.

I was changing course. How exciting was that! But at the same time, it was also daunting and stressful, and I felt very uncertain.

From CEO to caddie

So, where did I get the ideas, the inspiration and the insights I'd needed in order to change course *successfully*? I didn't want to repeat the mistakes I'd made before (in all areas of my life).

Bizarrely, these came from the most unlikely source – caddying at a golf course!

It all began with a suggestion from my wife. We watched a TV programme about the caddies at Scotland's 'The Old Course', St Andrews, and afterwards my wife said that maybe I should think about caddying as part of my recovery from the stroke.

She felt it would keep me fit, and give me the opportunity to meet the types of people I used to work with. Also, she thought it would be good for my confidence. (And, from her point of view, it would get me out of the house!)

I'd always loved golf and was a member of a famous club, The North Berwick Golf Club, which attracts thousands of players each year. It's a links course with a great location. Nestled next to the shores of the Firth of Forth, about 32 kilometres (20 miles) east of Edinburgh, it offers fantastic views of the beaches below, the Kingdom of Fife and the islands of the Firth of Forth – notably The Bass Rock.

It's also the 13th oldest golf course in the world – founded in 1832 – with a long and proud history. Altogether, it's a superb place to play golf, and it regularly hosts a number of prestigious events. So, I approached the caddie master and starter at the club, and with his help and support, I began caddying there in 2008.

Since then, I've caddied for doctors, lawyers, judges, pilots, venture capitalists, millionaires, billionaires, sports champions, bankers, truck drivers, politicians, entrepreneurs, investment managers, professors, senators, estate agents, brokers and CEOs.

There have been fathers, grandfathers, wives, sons and daughters; those for whom a trip to Scotland to play golf was small change, and others for whom it was the trip of a lifetime. I've met players from across the USA – Texas, North Carolina, South Carolina, New York, California, Boston, Florida, New Jersey, Chicago, Seattle, San Francisco and Denver – as well as from countries such as France, Canada, Australia, Germany, Denmark, Japan, Italy and England.

There have been golfers from the world's major cities, but also some from small towns and villages; those who'd been to Scotland many times previously, and others who were visiting for the first time.

As the years passed, I started to realize that, by spending five or six hours with these (usually) very successful people, I could share some of their experiences. I could pick up on the things they said, and the philosophies and beliefs they lived by which made them the people they were.

It was one of those golfers – Brad, a stockbroker from New York – who pointed this out to me: 'What a great opportunity you have – to see what makes these people tick,' he remarked. And he was right. What a privileged position I was in – I could learn how these successful people did things, hear about some of their life experiences and enjoy their stories. All by just chatting to them as I caddied!

So, let me pay tribute right here to all the golfers I've caddied for. I got many of the ideas, the insights and the inspiration I was looking for on how to change course from my conversations with them. They taught me many new things, reinforced other things I'd already known and challenged some of the ideas I believed were true but which turned out to be false.

Seven years on, through my experiences of being a CEO, a stroke survivor and a caddie, I've accumulated a wealth of ideas, methods, thoughts and philosophies on how to change course successfully.

And I've come to the following conclusion: changing course can be a fantastic opportunity, one in which new discoveries and positive outcomes will be constantly presented, despite the fact that the start of the road can be very daunting or stressful.

So, whether you've just lost your job, have decided that you want to do something completely different with your life, or are recovering from a health scare, this book has been designed to help you change course.

All of the people you'll read about are real: their names and where they live have been changed, to respect their privacy. In my years as a caddie, I've kept a private blog in which I've recorded all the insights, ideas and thoughts I've gained from caddying for some fascinating and remarkable people. It's from this blog that I've drawn the stories in this book.

This isn't an academic book, nor is it one that looks at the theory of changing course. Instead, it's a *practical handbook* – packed full of straightforward advice and thought-provoking and challenging ideas on how to take your life in a different direction. Hopefully, as I did, you'll find inspiration and wisdom in the stories of the people I've caddied for.

Seven years ago, I was forced to change course from my role as a CEO. Today I'm a caddie, but I'm also a non-executive director, a consultant, a joint founder of a charity and an author. I've achieved all this after having a stroke by applying the lessons, ideas, insights and beliefs contained in this book.

I wish you the best of luck on your journey in changing course.

PART 1

CHANGING COURSE FOUNDATION

Chapter 1

JUMP OUT OF BED

Love what you do

First of all, let me tell you about Mark from California, a guy who 'used to sell houses in The Valley' (his description, not mine).

Mark was a great golfer, so my job as his caddie was pretty easy. I wasn't spending time looking for his ball in the rough, so we talked a lot as we walked along the fairways. Over the first few holes, he told me about his family – especially his daughter and his wife, who'd joined him on his golf trip to Scotland.

This was my first clue that Mark was a bit different from most of the people I caddie for, who tend to come with friends. He was also different in another, more fundamental, way: he *loved* what he did for a living. He had a *passion* for it. He told me that he jumped out of bed every morning, looking forward to the day ahead.

And no, his job didn't involve saving lives, or working with the sick, the homeless or the poor. Mark renovated houses. And he loved it! For him, it was exciting. He felt it was his calling in life, his purpose.

He'd buy a house, hire the team needed to do it up and then manage the whole process. He even did a lot of the renovation work himself. Then he'd sell the house.

Mark *really* loved renovating houses, but *why*? Well, until two years previously, he'd spent 20 years at a very large real estate company in the USA, working his way up to senior executive level. The pay was good, as were the benefits, but the role was a stressful one, and this took its toll on his health and his personal relationships.

And, at the end of the day, it was just a job. A good, well-paid job, but nothing more.

Then, in the mid-noughties, the global financial crisis hit the USA. The country's property sector was badly affected, but Mark didn't lose his job. Instead, he decided to leave it voluntarily. He opted to give up his $200,000-plus salary and benefits.

So, what prompted this seemingly rash action? Mark told me it had been down to something that a close friend had told him after *his* job had been made redundant. He'd explained it to Mark like this: 'Now I have the excuse to do something that'll really make me happy; to do something I love. I still need to earn money, but now I can do something that I really want to do.'

Mark was hugely affected by his friend's new attitude. He'd always dreamed of having his own small business renovating houses, but had never done anything about it. But then he thought to himself: *why don't I finally do something I'll feel passionate about and love doing? How about making the dream a reality, just like my friend is about to do?*

So, at 52, Mark left the company where he'd worked for the previous two decades. When I met him, two years later, he was earning less than he used to – and the benefits weren't as good or as plentiful – but boy, was he happier, less stressed and more relaxed! And he was so passionate about the job he loves doing every day.

His relationships with his wife and daughter had improved – he took them on his golfing trips because he wanted to spend time with them, and they loved to join him. That wouldn't have happened while he was doing his old job, he said.

Mark told me that there was only one downside to his new life: he wished he'd changed course 10 years earlier.

A fantastic opportunity

So, if you want to hear some *positive* news when you're in a bad place, it's this: if you can change your thinking to, *at long last I have the opportunity to do something that I'm really passionate about*, good things *can* happen, as they did for Mark.

Of course, it may be very difficult to think like this when things aren't going well for you. But trust me, in changing the course of your life, you have an opportunity that most people don't have, or take – a chance to do something you'll *really love doing* – something that makes you jump out of bed in the morning, looking forward to the day ahead.

In reality, most working people have no passion for what they do every day, and they don't see a real purpose to it. They *dream* about doing something *else* with their lives – setting up their own business, writing a book, going back into full-time education, working for another company, moving abroad, becoming an artist…

But they don't *make* the change. Instead, they get stuck in the same job or role and feel trapped but unable to escape because of their commitments – from mortgages and bills to school fees and insurances. And, perhaps, it's also because they're afraid they'll fail, or are scared of losing the 'status' that comes with their current role.

But here's what the late, great Steve Jobs, US entrepreneur and co-founder of computer giant Apple, said about all of this:

'Your work is going to fill a large part of your life, and the only way to be truly satisfied is to do what you believe is great work, and the only way to do great work is to love what you do.'

Whether you've been forced to change course, or whether you're choosing to do it, you now have a chance to do something you've always wanted to – something you feel passionate about. You can finally embark on what you dream of doing but, for whatever reason, just haven't got around to.

I can imagine what's going through your mind now: *all this positive thinking is fine, but I still need to settle the bills, pay the mortgage and feed my family*. Yes, of course you do. But it's *perfectly possible* to do something you are passionate about and *still* meet your financial commitments.

You may find that you need to manage your money more carefully – perhaps cut back on big expenditures or even downsize to a smaller home – but if you *really* want to do something, you'll find ways to make it happen, and it might all just start by reading this book!

Spending time with Mark, and seeing the enthusiasm he had for his job, made me understand that to change course successfully, you need to find a career, a role, a job or a pastime that will fill you with excitement, and which you'll love doing. The benefits of doing this could be immense in terms of your happiness, your wellbeing and you relationships.

I've caddied for people from a wide range of backgrounds – from doctors to truck drivers – and I've noticed that while some seemed to be at ease with themselves, others had an aura of unhappiness about them. It wasn't until the round progressed and I got to know them better, that it became obvious that those people who were at ease with themselves, and with their life in general, were the ones who loved their roles or jobs.

These were people who'd been bankers but who now ran their own companies; teachers who'd gone back to university to retrain for another career; lawyers who'd decided to look after their children full time; accountants who'd given their time to charities; housewives who'd set up businesses from home; doctors who'd taken a year out to travel the world. People like Mark.

I've also met people – both as a caddie and as a CEO – who'd been forced to change course because of health issues. They were unable to do their original job or role any longer, but once they'd recovered as much as was possible, they went on to take up new and exciting roles that they were passionate about, regardless of their physical or cognitive impairments.

They ran companies, became trustees of national charities, set up new businesses, travelled the world and set up social enterprises.

As a CEO, I spent a lot of time with some extraordinary people – those who had, on paper, 'made it'. However, once I got to know them better – when they opened up to me over a beer or a meal – I was often surprised to learn that they dreamed of doing something completely different with their lives.

However, because of their financial commitments, and a fear of losing their status, they felt trapped. When I scratched the surface of their lives, I'd find that, although they *wished* they were doing something else, they *weren't doing anything about it*.

They'd stay on in the same role, getting progressively more unhappy, or frustrated or jaded. Their passion was long gone, and they'd come to dread Monday mornings, living only for the weekends.

This book will show you how *not* to be like those people. It'll show you how to be the person who jumps out of bed every morning, buzzing with enthusiasm for the day ahead. It'll show you how to change course successfully, like Mark did.

What makes you itch?

The first thing you need to do is realize that you can't do it alone. You're going to have to build a 'team' around you to provide help and support. And here's why. Nearly all big, and even most small, companies have a board of directors who help steer the business to success. They debate and make the big decisions about the company's strategy, and they also provide a sounding board for the CEO.

This is precisely what you need as you start out – a changing course board, or team. For this, you'll need a need a minimum of three (and a maximum of six) trusted friends, relatives or supporters who'll be willing and able to assist, guide, challenge and support you on your new path.

When I was forced to change course after my stroke, I had four people on my 'team' – my wife, my brother and two very close friends. Collectively, they gave me brilliant support, and came up with ideas, suggestions and brainwaves. In fact, they still do!

Your team will be the most important people in your life as you change direction, so you must trust them and listen to what they say. Talk to them about all the ideas, insights and suggestions contained in this book. You'll be amazed by the amount of feedback, contacts and information you'll receive in return.

Once your team is in place, your next step is to think about the roles in your current life that you're really *passionate* about. What do you *love* doing? If you can't think of anything ask yourself, what do I *dream* of doing? What do I imagine the future could be like if I did the things and took on the roles that I *really* wanted to? In the words of the twentieth-century philosopher Alan Watts: 'What do you desire? What makes you itch? What sort of a situation would you like?'

These are the things that you should now be doing as you go forwards and change course. These are the roles and occupations that should fill a large part of your day.

So, the first fundamental principle for changing course successfully is this: love what you do. This is applicable regardless of what it is that you decide to do as you change course: from starting your own business to working for a charity, becoming a full-time dad or going back into full-time education, to travelling the world.

However, you're probably wondering how you can be *sure* that the role or occupation you dream of doing, or are planning to do, will give you the feeling that Mark had? How do you *know* that you'll be 'jumping out of bed' every morning?

Well, while *love what you do* is a key principle, it's not the only one. It's connected to a second one, and together they will help you lay down a fantastic foundation for changing course successfully. Robert from Toronto showed me this second principle. Let me tell you about his business card.

Chapter 2

BLOODY HELL! GET EXCITED!

Do things that you feel make a difference

Most of the people I caddie for come to Scotland for one reason only – to play golf on some of the most historic, challenging and beautiful courses in the world. They're here for ten days or so, and play one round – sometimes two – every day, in all weather conditions.

When I chat to them during the game, the conversation is mainly about golf – the courses they've just played, the courses they're about to play. Almost all of them play a 'competition' with the people who are on the trip with them. For example, they will set up daily competitions, team competitions and an overall trip competition.

Robert from Toronto was typical in all these aspects. He was at 'my' club to play golf with seven of his friends from his golf club in Canada.

'Bloody hell, I'm excited!' he exclaimed as we stood on the 1st tee. 'I've been looking forward to this trip for ages.' This was the first round of 12 that he'd be playing 'in competition' with his friends, and in the evenings they were planning to relax over malt whiskies before enjoying some good Scottish food.

In fact, Robert was so excited about all this that he completely missed his first drive! To me, his enthusiasm was wonderful because it captured the essence of a great golf trip to Scotland. He was keen to chat to me all the way round the course – not only about his trip, but also about his career.

I discovered that he was a creative director at one of Toronto's largest advertising agencies, working on both national and global campaigns. And from the way he talked about his company and the people he worked with, I could tell that he *loved* what he did.

At the end of the round, Robert did something that people occasionally do when I caddie for them: he gave me his business card and said if I was ever in Toronto and fancied a game of golf, I should call him. When I got home, I looked at the business card and saw the following quote on the back of it:

'While some may see them as the crazy ones, we see genius. Because the people who are crazy enough to think they can change the world are the ones who do'. Then came the added words: '*Let us make a difference in your world.*'

I'd heard the quote before because it's part of a famous Apple advert from the 1990s called 'Think Different', but it still had a powerful impact on me. However, it was the last part of the card that really made me think, though: 'Let us make a difference in your world.'

Combine passion with purpose

Robert's business card reminded me of the second fundamental principle for changing course, which is this: whatever you're about to embark on, do it because you feel it will make a difference. If you can do that, your 'new' life will be far more fulfilling and exciting. It really will make you want to 'jump out of bed' every day!

Here's a question for you: when was the last time you got *really excited* about something? I don't mean having a meal at your favourite restaurant or buying a car. I mean something that consumed your thoughts over a period of time – weeks, months, or even years.

Something that made the hairs on the back of your neck stand up. Something that made you believe that, if you *did* it, you would truly be making a difference – not only to yourself but to the people around you, too. If you don't have that feeling now, I have some positive news for you.

Changing course is your opportunity to do something that will make a difference. It doesn't matter what that 'something' is – it could be a role, an occupation or a hobby. What's important is that you feel and believe that it's right, and that it has a purpose.

During my time as CEO of Company Net, our clients came from a wide range of sectors – from retail to manufacturing, from finance to charities, and from entertainment to the voluntary sector. I can honestly say that, whatever their business, the clients we loved working with most were those who had a real sense of purpose and a genuine belief that what they were doing was making a difference.

These companies, and the people who worked for them, had a pride in, and a passion for, what they did, and I believe this is one of the greatest things that changing course can give you.

Some people call this having a 'mission' or a 'goal'. Jason Fried, co-author of *Rework: Change the Way You Work Forever*, calls it 'making a dent in the universe'. I like that notion, but whatever *you* call it, just make sure you do things that you believe will make a difference.

This doesn't mean you should only do 'worthy' things, just the things that you really *believe* in – the ones that give you a *sense of purpose*.

In the early years of Company Net's existence, we were excited just to be running a company and having clients. And for a while that was fine. We kind of knew what we were trying to sell, but to be honest, we didn't know *why* we were doing it.

Then I started to get the feeling that our staff were unsettled – some were even leaving to work for our competitors. There were negative comments about how we were doing things, and I too began to question what we were doing. It seemed that we were going from one project to the next without any overall reason or purpose.

In truth, there was a lack of direction in the business, and little or no pride in what we were all about. For me, this hit home when a mentor posed a simple question that I just *couldn't* answer: 'What's the purpose of your company? What is its mission?'

This is a straightforward but telling question, and it's critical that you, too, can answer it as you change course. I've suggested that you search for something that you'll love doing, but you should also identify a *real purpose or mission.*

So, if I were to ask you: 'What's the overall purpose of what you're about to embark on?', how would you respond? If your answer fails to give you a feeling of dignity and significance, and if you believe that what you want to do would *not* make a difference to people's lives (especially your own), I'd strongly recommend that you think again about your chosen route.

This is exactly what we did at Company Net. I came to the conclusion that I wanted to have a shared sense of purpose among our people that what we did was making a difference – to our clients, to our suppliers and to ourselves. We conducted a number of meetings with them all to find out what excited them most about what the company did. I also asked the same question of myself.

It turned out that the two aspects of our work that most excited everyone were 'innovation' and 'discovery'. We believed that if we could give our clients *innovative* solutions that led them to new *discoveries* about how they could work better, we would be making a real difference to everyone involved.

With that purpose in mind, we were able to agree a set of values the company would adopt in doing innovative work, and these were then applied to *everything* we did. We got into the habit of ensuring that in any new projects we were presenting to our clients, there would be an innovative solution – one that gave them a new discovery about how *they* could improve their way of working.

In time, we started to feel really passionate about the company again, and to really love what we did. True, we weren't saving lives, but we were making a difference to our clients. We had found a *sense of purpose*, and I was incredibly proud of what we were achieving.

Moving to a role or a job that you feel makes a difference is one of the best opportunities presented to you when changing course. But make sure that whatever you're planning to do gives you a sense of dignity and respect, and that it feels significant.

What's your mission?

While I was in hospital recovering from my stroke, I shared a ward with three other men, all of whom had suffered a stroke. One, a retired general practitioner (GP) in his eighties called Hamish, had a big effect on me. As we talked together during those few days, he showed me the benefits of living a life that gives a feeling of making a difference.

Now, I know what you're thinking – obviously a medical practitioner will feel that he's made a difference. Which is true, but Hamish communicated something else to me – that he'd had a real calling to be a particular *type* of doctor.

After his training, Hamish chose to work in a doctor's practice on a small group of islands off the Highlands of Scotland, and he remained there for the rest of his professional life. He told me that he'd loved his job because he'd been able to care for his patients from 'cradle to grave' – many of them were born on the islands, and lived, worked and died there, too.

Hamish told me that he could have moved to the Scottish mainland for a better-paid position, but he'd always believed that doing so would rob him of the feeling he got from being a GP on the islands – the sense that he was making a significant difference, not only in the lives of others, but in his own.

As I chatted with Hamish, and watched him with his family, I got the impression of a man who was completely at peace with himself, despite his health issues. He'd certainly made a 'dent in the universe'.

This is what *you* are trying to achieve when you change course. Do that thing you'll love doing, but make sure that it also gives you a feeling that you're making a difference.

This is your mission and your purpose – the 'dent' you'll make in the universe. And, like Robert, 'Bloody hell! I'm excited!' is exactly how you should feel when you've worked out what it is that you really want to do.

Okay, I'm guessing that you are screaming at me now: 'Yes, I agree! Why should I spend the rest of my life doing something I *don't* really like doing? I get it!'

But how do you *begin* the process of finding out what you'll really love doing? Well, let me tell you about another golfer I had the pleasure of meeting – Gerry from Detroit in the USA – who showed me the third principle that completes the foundation you need to lay if you're going to make a success of changing course.

Chapter 3

BE LIKE DETROIT

Focus on your strengths

I think that Gerry from Detroit should have been in advertising rather than investment banking. Not because advertising is, arguably, a more acceptable career than banking these days, but because of the way he described his home city.

Gerry and I were standing on the 2nd tee on a glorious spring day. The tide was right out and the beach below looked perfect. As we were waiting to tee off, he asked me if I'd ever been to Detroit. I told him I'd only spent a few hours at its airport, waiting for a connecting flight.

I then admitted that my overall impression of the city wasn't a particularly positive one. Based purely on certain films I'd seen – *Gran Torino*, *8 Mile* – and articles I'd read in newspapers, I believed that Detroit was a bit run-down, especially after the collapse of the car industry. I thought it was a bit violent, and definitely unsafe.

Gerry told me that I wasn't alone in holding that view, as most people share it. Then he looked at me, pointed a finger and intoned in a mock deep voice: 'Detroit, focusing on its strengths, not its weaknesses!'

He went on to explain that, by 'focusing on its strengths', Detroit is *changing*. The city is becoming more vibrant, more confident. More businesses are starting up. New houses and suburbs are being built. There's a blossoming arts scene. The city's leaders are incredibly motivated to make the place successful again.

It's true that Detroit is still facing serious issues, he admitted, but the way out of them is for the city to focus on its strengths, and to use them as a way of developing new opportunities for its citizens. Gerry was as passionate about this approach as he was about his home city, and suggested that the next time I was planning a trip to the USA that included a connecting trip via Detroit, I should take at least a day out to visit the city and see what it has to offer. 'You'll be surprised by what you find,' he assured me.

And Gerry would know because, as an investment banker, he invested in Detroit.

Identify your innate talents

One of the first things you need to do when you're looking to change course to do something you'll love – something that'll give you a purpose – is focus on your strengths rather than your weaknesses.

It's a simple, but great, concept! And what's even better is the fact that *everyone*, including you, has strengths. Or, to put it another way, we all have *innate talents.*

However, actually *identifying* these talents can be tricky. Much of what you're taught at school, in college or university, or in your employment – from your first job to the one you're currently doing – has tended to focus on just the opposite.

The education system in the UK is traditionally exam-based. If you have a talent for remembering facts, writing essays or solving scientific equations, you're likely to do well. If not, in the main, you'll be seen as an academic failure. This was certainly the case for me!

I'd bet that your current employer (or the last one) employed you on the basis of your CV and one, maybe two, interviews. And here's the key question: throughout your academic and professional career, has anyone seriously looked at what you're *really* good at doing – the things that come *naturally* to you?

By this, I don't mean the things that you're *skilled* at – skills are things you *learn* to do, like riding a bike, driving a car or using a particular piece of software. Nor do I mean the things you're *knowledgeable* about – knowledge is something you gain from reading, from having new experiences, from watching TV or from listening to others.

Even more importantly, do ***you*** know what your innate talents are?

Let me give you some examples of what I mean:

- You walk into a room where a meeting is in progress and, very quickly, you pick up on the atmosphere. If the meeting has been going badly, you are able to *feel* the tension in the air. The key here is that you sense this tension without anyone actually saying anything. *You have a talent for empathy.*

- Others in that meeting may be completely oblivious to the tension. However, there's one person who's desperate for everyone to reach a decision. They have a talent for getting things done quickly. *A talent for action.*

- Lastly, there's a person who's getting stressed that the agenda is changing and that the meeting is now covering lots of new subjects. That person has a talent for concentrating on one thing at a time. *A talent for focus.*

If you aren't using *your* innate talents, the chances are that you aren't enjoying your job, or role, as much as you could be. And it's my guess that you won't be *loving* it. The majority of people in work today are skilled at what they do, and they're likely to be knowledgeable about it, too, but unfortunately, many of them are in jobs or roles that aren't employing their natural talents.

The third and final principle in the foundation for changing course is this: focus most of your time and effort on using your talents.

I made plenty of bad decisions when I was the CEO of Company Net, but one of the *good* things I did was to apply this philosophy about innate talents and strengths to my staff and myself.

For many years, I recruited people based only on their knowledge and skills. However, after a mentor highlighted the fact that people perform far better in roles in which they are using their talents for most of the time, I decided to find out what my staff (and I) were naturally good at.

We utilized an online programme – backed up with some consultancy from a company that specialized in it – that identified the top five talents of everyone in the company. The results were remarkable, both for the business and for individual members of staff. We were now able to put people in roles that *we* knew, and *they* knew, best suited their talents.

It gave everyone a really good understanding of what they should be doing with their lives and their careers. Some staff changed roles within the company, while others gained more confidence and began to thrive in their existing role. Other people moved on to careers elsewhere when they realized that they weren't using their talents for most of the time with us.

On a personal level, I found that I could spend more of my time doing activities I was innately good at, and delegate those tasks in which I had limitations. For everyone involved with the company, the practice of focusing time on the things they were innately good at was inspiring and incredibly motivating.

The online tool we used is part of a method developed by The Gallup Organization. Through interviews with 1.7 million professionals from various fields and roles – executives, salespeople, teachers, doctors, lawyers, students, administrators, manual labourers and nurses, to name but a few – Gallup were able to develop a way of identifying people's top talents and strengths. They called it the 'Strengths Finder', and to date it has been used by millions of people around the world.

Find help and resources

So, if you don't know what *your* innate talents are, I'd advise you to spend some time identifying them before you make any big decisions about changing course. Your aim should be to move into a role where you can use your talents and your strengths for most of the time, because only then will you create the possibility that you'll love doing that role.

It's one of the most fundamental principles for identifying a job or a role that you'll love, and where you feel you are making a difference – do something where you use most of your talents, for most of the time.

There's a huge range of tools, books and online assessments and methods to help you find your talents and strengths. One of these is the Gallup 'Strengths Finder', which we used at Company Net. This tool is available for purchase at *www.gallupstrengthscenter.com* and will help you to identify your top five strengths.

Additionally, or alternatively, you can buy the Strengths Finder book published by Gallup Press (*www.strengthsfinder.com*). This gives you information about the tool and its history, and contains far more detail about talents and strengths. It's a brilliant book.

If this all feels a bit formal, or if you don't like doing this kind of assessment, a simple way of uncovering your talents is to just ask your friends and family – those who are closest to you – what *they* think your strengths are.

By this, I mean the things they've observed you are naturally good at. Don't ask them about your knowledge and your skills, but about your innate talents. For example, they might point out the following things about you, or something similar:

- You're really adaptable and can spin many plates at once.
- You're fantastic at communicating, whether one-to-one or in front of a big crowd.
- You're driven to get things done.
- You have a wonderful ability to get the most out of people.
- You dislike conflict and try to bring people together.
- You love thinking and pondering about things.
- You want to be number one in everything that you take on.

If you really think about it, you'll probably find that *you* know exactly what you're naturally good at. So, along with considering what your family and friends tell you, ask yourself which aspects of your current job, role or hobby fill you with excitement. In which areas do you get the most positive feedback from others; which tasks do you feel 'really comfortable' doing?

Those are the areas in which you are using your talents.

After the stroke, I had significant cognitive impairment in a number of areas. I still do. However, it became apparent fairly quickly that my natural talents had remained largely intact: I was still bursting with ideas and keen to put them into practice; I could still pick up the 'mood' of a room very quickly; and I could still see how to achieve potential outcomes by connecting up ideas and people.

My limitations, however, were far more pronounced than they had been before the stroke: organizing and planning my week was very challenging; focusing on one thing, one role, even for a short while was very difficult; and scenario planning was virtually impossible.

To see if I'd retained my talents, though, I did the 'Strengths Finder' assessment a few years after my stroke. It was five years since I'd first done it, yet the results were unchanged! My talents were the same as they'd been before the stroke.

All of this only served to emphasize that I should focus more than ever on developing my strengths. When I did that, I was able to achieve far more than if I'd tried to do the things I knew I had limitations in. I still do this today. And the results remain the same: whenever I focus on my strengths, I achieve more, I'm less tired, it feels natural and I really enjoy doing it.

Gerry, with that one statement about Detroit 'focusing on its strengths', helped me to remember, and to reinforce, something I'd learned as a CEO.

So, we've looked in depth at the three *Changing Course* principles, which should form the foundation of everything you do as you change course:

Love what you do + Do things that you believe make a difference + Focus most of your time and efforts on using your talents.

But you'll also need to develop and maintain a particular *mindset* throughout your journey. In the next section I'll be showing you how. First, though, let me introduce you to Bill from South Dakota.

PART 2

CHANGING COURSE MINDSET

Chapter 4

BELIEVE

What you believe determines whether or not you'll succeed

Over the years, both in business and as a caddie, I've noticed that people generally fall into one of two camps – those who see the glass as 'half full' and those who see it as 'half empty'. The optimists versus the pessimists.

Bill from South Dakota was definitely in the pessimists' camp. He was in his late 60s and still worked full-time running a manufacturing company. This was his third trip to Scotland but the first to play 'my' course.

As we set out, the course was in perfect condition; the greens were immaculate, the rough and the fairways looked stunning. It was a lovely day, with little wind and blue skies. The tide was right up and it was possible to hear and see the waves hitting the rocks below on the beach.

After a few holes, I started to notice something about Bill: he kept beating himself up. He'd hit a great shot and then the next one might be poor, but it was his poor shots that he talked about – all the time. He got annoyed with himself – telling me exactly what he was doing wrong but then doing that same thing again and getting even more angry.

He kept saying how bad he was at golf – that he didn't know *why* he played – and gave the impression that he'd rather be anywhere other than on the golf course. And all of this during perfect conditions for the game!

For me, watching and listening to Bill was a strange experience. I reckon that at least half of his shots were in fact good, but he never talked about those. Unless, that is, I'd just said 'great shot', whereupon he'd reply: 'It won't last. Just watch the next one.' And, of course, he'd then hit a bad shot and off he'd go with the negative comments.

I found it all fascinating. He was just *waiting* to fail, and because of that he wasn't appreciating the natural beauty around him or the fact that he was with his friends, playing one of the world's best golf courses. He was blind to it all because of his 'glass half empty' mindset and his belief that he wouldn't play well.

If you are considering changing course, or are being forced to, having a mindset like Bill's will make it very difficult for you to make a success of it. The problem with having a negative mindset is that you'll always be waiting for things to go wrong. You'll be convinced that, because things have gone wrong in the past, they are likely to go wrong in the future.

Switch to positive

But here's a fact about changing course – you'll have to face challenges every single day. And things might go wrong. Sometimes they'll go wrong regardless of what you do, and at other times you'll make mistakes. Things will also happen that are outside your control. What's absolutely crucial, though, is how you *deal* with these challenges. This is undoubtedly one of the main issues facing you on your new path.

If you have a 'glass half empty' mindset, you will find, like Bill, that things *will* go wrong all the time. Because you believe this, they simply will. What *can* go wrong *will* go wrong! What's worse is that you believe you can't do new things, or take risks, or grab exciting opportunities, because you'll fail. Having a negative mindset is very dangerous when you are changing course.

Interestingly, though, the equation also works in reverse. Change to a positive mindset – one in which you tell yourself that you *can* do something, that you *could* take a risk and do something new – and, strangely enough, you'll find ways to achieve things.

So, if you're to do something completely new in your life, you really must *believe* that you can succeed. You must embark on this new journey in the sure and certain belief that it will work. You must understand that when things go wrong or are difficult, the situation is only temporary and it will improve.

Try to foster a belief that things *will* work out for the best, even though it might not seem possible at the time. If you *don't* have this belief, this mindset, it is unlikely that you will succeed in your new venture.

The great US industrialist Henry Ford knew this. He said: 'Whether you think you can or you think you can't, you are right.' How powerful is that statement? A belief in something is contagious and self-fulfilling, as I saw with Bill. Even though he was a good golfer, with a great swing, his belief that he would fail – that he would hit a bad shot – made it happen more often than it should have done.

You need to understand that when you are changing course, the belief you have about something creates a *momentum* to keep you doing it. A positive attitude will propel you forwards; a negative attitude will hold you back.

Understanding this is even more important if you've been forced to change course – through losing your job or having a health scare, for example – rather than choosing to do so. Whatever the reason, it's really important be aware of this:

Whatever life has thrown at you, the key to making a success of your new path is how you* react *to everything, what you decide to* focus *your attention on, and, ultimately, what you* believe *is now possible.

If you think that no-one will employ you because your job has been made redundant, the chances are that they won't. If you believe that, because you've been a parent of young children for eight years, the odds of you setting up your own business are well-nigh zero, then they will be.

Perhaps you have a health issue and, whilst you've recovered as much as is possible, it still prevents you from doing the job you once did. If you believe that there's no other role or occupation you could take up instead – well, there won't be. In all these cases, your beliefs will be proved correct, and you'll reinforce them every time you think along those lines.

So, whatever has prompted you to change course, try to adopt the view that, even though things may be difficult, it's the *choices* that only you can make that'll take you to a new and better place. You must believe that it's up to *you*: it's your choices, your decisions and your belief that you can do new things.

Believe in yourself

For a while after my stroke I believed that the course of my new life was pretty terrible. In fact, my family, my friends and my company believed this, too! I'd had to resign from my job, and I wasn't able to communicate at all well.

Life seemed very poor indeed, and I had no idea what I was going to do in the future. For a time, I believed that I wouldn't do *anything* meaningful ever again, and that was a truly frightening thought.

But then two things happened and my outlook changed. The first was something one of my fellow directors said to me, around six months after the stroke:

> *'Even though you can't be the CEO again, you have other choices. You just need to believe that you can do other things, new things.*
>
> *'You've done it many times before – setting up an internet company when you had no technology skills, for example! You just have to believe that there will be new opportunities for you.'*

He was right: I *did* have other choices. And that notion really started to fire my imagination. It was all about the *choices* I would make as I moved forwards – focusing on the strengths I still had and then applying them to the countless opportunities that were out there for me. I just needed to have more confidence! And I did. The more I believed in myself the more I started to see new opportunities and choices everywhere.

The second thing was caddying – one of those 'new opportunities'. My wife believed it would help my confidence, and she was right: my confidence soared because I found I could still relate to the successful people I caddied for, and what they did. I found the stories they told me motivating and inspiring, and their advice and insights were invaluable.

I started to believe that, for me, caddying was more than just carrying a golf bag for a player and giving advice about the course. It was also an opportunity to learn new things that I could apply to my own life. It could give me ideas about changing course and starting again.

This, ultimately, led to a belief that, with all these experiences I was enjoying, a publisher might be interested in a story about the CEO who became a caddie, and a book about changing course. I stuck to that belief.

So, today, as I sit and write, I realize that the stroke gave me the opportunity to do things I'd previously believed weren't possible. Things that are *completely* new to me – like writing this book!

Immediately after the stroke, just after I came out of hospital, I kept a video diary. In one entry I'm sitting with my daughter, then aged eight, trying to read one of my youngest son's books. It was one of those A, B, C books, and I just *couldn't* read it. For example, I knew I was *seeing* an apple in the 'A' chapter, but I couldn't *say* what it was. That's what the stroke had done to my brain.

However, seven years on from a time when I couldn't even say what a bear or a pig was, I've managed to write a book. And it was my unswerving belief – after those early doubts – that I *could* write a book, despite my circumstances, which allowed me to do it, and everything else I've achieved since my stroke.

So, regardless of the cards life has dealt you, if you believe you can change course for something better, you will get there. If you're thinking of doing something new in your life, you need to really *believe* that you can do it. Apply the principles outlined in the Foundation section and the momentum you'll get from having this positive mindset will be incredibly powerful.

However, there's a crucial 'but'! Make sure that the decisions you make about changing course are what I call 'intelligent risks'. Let me explain what I mean by that with the inspiration I got from caddying for Kerry.

Chapter 5

BUNGEE JUMPING IN NEW ZEALAND

Take intelligent risks

Recently, a big event happened in my family. We took my eldest son off to university for the first time. According to some of my older and wiser friends, my wife and I were about to enter a new stage in our family life. We've been through the engagement stage (*the blissful stage*), the young married couple stage (*the no arguments stage*), and the young parent stage (*the no sleep stage*).

We are currently in the teenager stage (*the nightmare stage*) and are embarking on the first stage of our children leaving home (*the getting our lives back stage*).

I made a similar observation about these stages of family life to Kerry from San Diego when I caddied for her. I told her that my children are starting to leave home and that, when they've gone, my wife and I will have lots of 'new' free time to do other things with our lives while we still can.

This assumes, of course, that we've not spent all our money on another stage which may well occur – the one where our children move back home after graduating because they can't find a job (*nightmare stage two*)!

Kerry understood what I meant by these stages, as she'd gone through them with her own children. She was an incredibly inspiring person to be around, especially when she revealed why she was playing golf in Scotland.

She told me how, eight years previously, her husband had died, leaving her to bring up her two teenage children, then aged 16 and 17. When the youngest child left home for university, Kerry was determined not to feel sorry for herself – there'd been enough grief in the house when her husband had died. She was determined to do new things, and was willing to take some risks in doing them.

So, with the encouragement of her children, Kerry booked herself on a two-month trip to Asia, Australia and New Zealand – places she'd always wanted to visit. And it was in New Zealand that she did something that shocked even her. A bungee jump!

Why did she do it? Because she'd wanted to try something different. She'd wanted to have new experiences related to that stage of her life, after the death of her husband and her children leaving home. For her, it felt natural to do a bungee jump. 'Every 54-year-old woman should try it!' she said, laughing.

After that first holiday, Kerry promised herself that, every year, she'd take a trip which would allow her to visit places she'd never been – and do something different while she was there. As part of her sixth major world trip, she was playing golf, sightseeing and travelling around Scotland and Ireland.

I really admire people like Kerry, who take the opportunity to introduce new things into their lives, even though they are dealing with major, life-changing events. Kerry felt that the risks associated with her trips were easily outweighed by the positive experiences she got out of them, and it seemed to me that she was right.

She wasn't just *thinking* or *talking* about travelling the world and seeking out exciting new activities, she was taking a risk and actually *doing* it – and this is an essential mindset to adopt and apply when you are changing course.

In the last chapter, I talked about having a positive mindset, but remember this:

A belief is only powerful if it turns into an action. So many people have dreams and ideas about doing something completely different with their lives. They talk to their partners and friends about it. They think about it constantly. But they don't actually do it.

They may have a strong belief that what they'd rather be doing *could* work out, but for whatever reason, they just don't take the risk and put it into action.

If you are currently performing a job or a role that you don't love – or one that you feel doesn't make a difference or use your talents for most of the time – let me share this brilliant insight from Albert Einstein: 'A ship is always safe at the shore, but that is not what it is built for.'

If this is the position you are in, you are like that ship. You need to understand that you are *meant* to be doing something else – and I'd guess that you probably know that already. You were *built* to do other things, and you need to change course.

But *how* do you do it? How do you turn the belief into a reality?

For me it was easy. I had no choice: I just had to get on with my new life. A very good friend of mine has said more than once that he is envious of me because I'm taking on new roles and doing new things while he is still 'stuck', as he puts it, in his (very well-paid) job. Obviously, he's not envious that I had a stroke, but he'd like to be tackling new challenges, too, and that's how he views my change of course.

Choose the right risks

This is one of the big positives if you are *forced* to change course – you *have* to do new things because there's just no other choice. For me, there was no great risk in doing something new, because I couldn't perform my previous role. It's far more difficult to *choose* to do something new. That takes a different type of courage.

So, how do you become like Kerry, or the other people I've caddied for who have changed course? How do you decide that you *will* travel the world, or set up a new business, or go back to university, or leave your job? How do you finally summon up the courage and actually *do* something completely new in your life; something that changes the course of it significantly?

Well, it all boils down to risk and reward.

There are two types of risk that you can take: daft risks and intelligent risks.

- Daft risks: with these, your anticipated outcome is negative and the potential upside is very limited.

- Intelligent risks: with these, your anticipated outcome is positive and the potential downside is very limited. Intelligent risks are the ones you should be going for when you're changing course.

Going back to Einstein's analogy, if you're not putting into action your desire to do something new in your life, you are like the ship at the shore. Deciding *not* to change course is therefore a daft risk to take. The anticipated outcome will be that, for the foreseeable future, you'll *remain* unhappy and unfulfilled. The potential upside is that you'll maintain the same standard of living. Are you really happy with that outcome?

Opting to continue on the same path that you've been following for years isn't a *neutral* decision. It's a big risk to take – and it's probably a daft risk with a big downside and little upside.

Changing course, however, is an intelligent risk to take. But whatever it is that you plan to do, you need to ensure that:

- You know you'll love doing it.
- You know it will give you a real sense that you are making a difference. And you have support, either from family or friends (preferably both), to do it.
- You firmly believe in this new job, role or pastime, and it will be using your strengths for most of the time.

Taking the intelligent risk to change course will be life changing. The potential downside is limited, but the potential upside is virtually unlimited. *This* is the risk you should be taking.

Of course, it's up to you to really examine what the downsides would be if you took the intelligent risk to do something new. You might lose income, for example; you might have to find a new job or move to a smaller home. Even then, if you really think about it and talk to your close friends, or your 'board', you may well find there's a strategy to either lessen or wipe out those potential downsides.

And even if the downsides *do* happen, the positive outcomes almost certainly will outweigh the negatives. Try to foster a mindset that's accepting of the fact that you'll make mistakes sometimes – and the wrong decisions – but in so doing, you'll gain new knowledge, connections and experiences that will be of significant benefit, and stand you in good stead for the future.

I'd go further and say this:

If you are not actively taking intelligent risks by seeking, creating and acting on opportunities that'll allow you to change course, you are very likely exposing yourself to more serious risks in the long term.

It no longer becomes just a daft risk to maintain the status quo: it becomes a very *serious* daft risk. By not taking the intelligent risk that you know you should, you open yourself up to a situation where you're not in control – someone or something else is. And in the long term, that's a recipe for unhappiness, stress and potential bitterness.

My experiences in business and in caddying have shown me the intelligent risks that some people take, and the positive upsides they derived from taking them. I've met numerous people whose lives have been *transformed* by taking intelligent risks. These are people who've set up their own companies, left big corporations to work for charities, opted to become a full-time parent, or travelled the world, like Kerry.

When I talked to these people about what they do now, it was obvious that they were fired up, excited and proud of what they've achieved. They took intelligent risks and the positive outcomes have been life-changing.

You can be like them: you just need to believe you can do it. Weigh up the risks, and if they are intelligent, and right for you, then go for it.

Be sure though, that when you come to take those intelligent risks it's the 'real' you who is taking them. What do I mean by that? Well, get ready to meet Niki.

Chapter 6

WHERE'S WALLY?

Be yourself

When my children were young, they had a series of picture books which they loved called *Where's Wally?* The concept was simple and clear. Wally, the main character, appears only once in each of the double-page illustrations of various locations. However, he's surrounded by hundreds of other Wally lookalikes.

The fun begins when you try to find Wally, because he blends in so well with the other characters. He doesn't stand out from the crowd, but his distinctive red-and-white striped shirt, bobble hat and glasses make him *a little* easier to recognize. Looking for Wally is really addictive, and the books provided great entertainment for my children, as well as occasional peace in the house for me and my wife!

Niki from Los Angeles was the complete opposite of Wally. Rather than trying to blend into the crowd, she stuck out. The moment I was introduced to her on the 1st tee, I knew how our time together would be: I was going to have a lot of fun caddying for her; she'd be a true extrovert; and I'd never lose sight of her because of the way she was dressed.

Niki had come to Scotland with seven friends, and boy, was she determined to enjoy herself! As soon as we'd teed off and were walking up the first fairway, she was jumping and yelling in excitement. She was wearing a bright pink and blue outfit which I'm sure would have glowed in the dark, and she hardly stopped to take a breath when she was talking – which was most of the time.

Fun, loud, brash, colourful and full of energy, she was great to caddie for. And she was, without doubt, completely different from the majority of the people I caddie for, most of whom wear a similar style of traditional golf attire and behave in a reserved manner on the golf course.

I got on well with Niki, and so I mentioned this difference to her. She laughed and said that I wasn't the first person to say this. As she bounced off down the fairway she called out:

'You've just got to be who you are – wear what you want, be true to yourself and don't conform. It's okay to be yourself.'

I wasn't surprised to learn, later in the round, that Niki was the CEO of a large new-media agency. She built websites, advised on social media and was a regular speaker at conferences on all things digital. She told me that she was successful in business because her clients 'bought' her – her energy, ideas and beliefs – when they engaged with her company.

'I just try to be genuine and say it as I see it – whatever that is!' she explained. 'And clients, in the main, love that. My agency just seems to stand out from the crowd.'

As I said, the complete opposite of Wally.

Your 'second chance'

Niki's assertion that it's okay to be yourself is so important to take on board when you are making changes in your life. Changing course will allow you to *rediscover* the 'real you' by ripping out all the things you've gathered over the years that don't feel genuine.

You now have an opportunity to examine views and opinions that you've accumulated or formulated over the course of your life but which you don't actually believe. You have a chance to stop conforming and just 'going along with the crowd', and to spend your time doing things that you really enjoy.

Accepting that it's okay to be yourself can be extremely liberating, and changing course gives you the platform and the impetus for doing this. It's a new beginning, a fresh start. In fact, it's a *second chance* to be the person you actually *want* to be.

I would imagine that you were in this position at some earlier stage in your life – perhaps when you were around 18, when you went off to university or college, or started your first job. You had all those ideas and beliefs about what you wanted to achieve in life, but at some point along the road you started to conform and take on jobs or roles that you'd never have imagined yourself doing when you were young.

Maybe, too, you started to form opinions that you didn't *really* believe in – it was just what the 'crowd' did. Perhaps you started doing things because they were the easiest route to take: not because you loved doing them, or because they gave you a purpose. You conformed. You followed the crowd. And like Wally, you blended in.

But changing course allows you to alter that. It allows you to accept that it's okay to be *you* again. It means that whoever you are, whatever you're planning to do, and whatever your dreams are for the future, *you will be your true self.* And that's okay.

In fact, it's far more than that. It means you'll be living with integrity in everything that you do. And living with integrity will bring fulfilment and meaning to your life.

So yes, it is okay to be yourself.

Most people don't get the opportunity to say that. They know that the role or job they do doesn't allow it. In their hearts and in their minds, they may be desperate to change course, but they don't do it. They continue with things that don't give them any real feelings of satisfaction, worth or joy. They blend in and conform.

The businessman-turned-painter

Recently, I bumped into a former client I'd once known quite well. Back then, he was a director of an insurance company and Company Net did work for him. He was always very friendly and pleasant, but I remember the rather unusual nature of our meetings. He'd always bring lots of people to them – five or six was typical – but hardly anyone contributed anything, apart from the director himself.

I noticed too, that his team were all dressed in very similar clothes – dark suits and white shirts for the men, blue/black skirts and white blouses for the women. When I attended meetings at his company's head office, I'd look up into the atrium where the reception was located and see the windows of the many meeting rooms on the many floors. Two things always struck me – first, that there were *so* many people in these different meetings. What on earth did they all do? And secondly, everyone was dressed exactly the same.

So, when I met this director seven year later, I was hugely surprised to see that he looked *completely* different. He'd grown a beard and was wearing jeans and a T-shirt. It was a weekday lunchtime at a formal restaurant where a lot of business people go, and he was meeting with some former colleagues from the insurance company. They were all wearing suits.

As we chatted, I discovered that his job had been made redundant three years previously. But, rather than trying to find another role in insurance, he'd decided to take up painting again – portraits and landscapes in a very modern style. He told me that he'd always loved painting but, as he said: 'For 25 years, I was tied to my work and had no real time to paint. Redundancy freed me from those ties.'

He now makes his living by painting, and, having checked out his work on his website, I believe he should have done it many years ago. He was finally being himself and the results were amazing.

Both the businessman-turned-painter and Niki seemed to me to have a sense of freedom from the constraints that the modern world puts on people: freedom from the pressure to conform. They appeared to be okay with who they were, and about what they were doing with their lives.

Both of them oozed such a sense of freedom and confidence in what they were doing, it gave me this insight:

Changing course can bring back the freedom to become the person you've always wanted to be, and to accept that this is okay.

I think this holds true even if you are being forced to change course. As I found out, that freedom is still there, *if you want it*. You'll need support, help and ideas from your friends and your family to achieve it, but it's always there.

So, going back to Wally, try not to blend in and follow the crowd – stand out and be the person you're meant to be. Get excited about the fact that it's okay to be that person. See changing course for what it is – a chance to be you! If you do this, you'll be like Niki, bouncing along in your new life, full of energy and purpose.

But it won't all be plain sailing as you change course. There will be challenges and setbacks, and how you view these will be crucial to your success. It was partly down to Steve from New England that I understood this.

Chapter 7

THE GUYS FROM GOOGLE

Go forwards not backwards

I would say that a significant proportion of the people I caddie for are seriously wealthy – they fly first-class, stay in the top hotels and dine in the finest restaurants. Then there are the super-rich. These people have their own jets and fly directly from the USA to Scotland, non-stop... and hire a country house rather than staying in a hotel.

Steve, from New England, was in the super-rich category. He'd flown in on his private jet with some friends to play golf over seven days. Then he was going to fly his friends home again. All 12 of them!

Steve was incredibly friendly, and a nice guy to be around. As we chatted, I found out that he was a venture capitalist and his specialism was investing in technology companies with innovative and ground-breaking products.

He asked me how long I'd been a caddie, and I explained that this was only my second year. Then I told him about my time as the CEO of an internet and web development company, and about the stroke. He seemed genuinely interested and asked me many questions about both situations.

One of the things I admitted to Steve was that I really didn't know what I was going to be able to do in my life, apart from caddying, or what the future had in store for me. At that point I was still, in many ways, longing for my old life. Steve then told me a fascinating story about himself that he thought I'd find helpful.

Back in the 1990s, he'd founded his own venture capital firm and was looking to make investments in technology start-ups. It was the beginning of the 'dot com' craze and he was inundated with business plans and requests for meetings with potential companies. Everyone, it seemed, had an internet idea that would make Steve millions!

One meeting that he still remembered vividly was with the founders of Google – Sergey Brin and Larry Page. At that time, Google would have been defined as a start-up company. It had few employees and little income, but it did have great and innovative technology for searching the internet.

Brin and Page were looking for an investment from Steve's company to help take Google to the next stage of the company's growth, and to capitalize on the ground-breaking technology they'd developed. They presented their business plan to Steve and his team and then outlined how much money they were looking for.

The investment required, in venture capital terms, was relatively small, but in return, Brin and Page were willing to offer Steve a significant percentage of Google. 'We are talking a big stake,' Steve told me. But, for a number of reasons, his company decided not to invest. He shook hands with the two entrepreneurs, and wished them all the best with Google.

Steve stopped walking for a moment, looked directly at me and said: 'Today, Google is worth billions – many, many billions. I would have had a significant share in those billions. But I don't.'

He went on: 'So, you must be wondering whether I scream at myself in the mirror every day, and say: "You bloody idiot, why did you make that decision?" (He was right, I was!)

'Well, I don't, and that's because I believe in the philosophy "it was meant to be". I wasn't *meant* to invest in Google. Simple as that! At the time that I met Brin and Page, it was the right decision. That's what I strongly believe. I don't do hindsight – the "what if" scenario.

'I just move on with my life and accept the decisions I've made. I don't regret them, I just learn from them. Funnily enough, two years on from that meeting, I got the opportunity to invest in a similar type of technology, which I did. It, like Google, turned out to be incredibly successful. I did very well from that,' he said with a smile.

Steve then said something that had a huge impact on me:

'Life goes forwards, not backwards. Don't think about or focus on what might have been. Instead, look out for the new opportunities and experiences that will be out there for you going forwards.'

You see, one of the challenges you'll face when you change course is that some of the time you'll wish you could get your old life back. Or you'll wish that you could reverse some of the decisions you've made.

This is more likely to happen if you've been forced to change course. You'll start to question *why* these difficult things are happening in your life. You'll get annoyed with yourself, or those around you, about certain events and outcomes. You might even question the fairness of life itself.

But, even if you chose to change course and are excited about the future, when things get difficult (which they *will*), it's inevitable that you'll start to look back on the roles or occupations you had before with some longing and affection. You might start to beat yourself up about the decisions you've made, and believe now, with hindsight, that they were foolish or plain wrong.

This is a real challenge, but whatever happens, you should make every effort to avoid doing this. Don't linger on regrets and 'what may have been' scenarios. By all means celebrate your memories, and look back on the experiences you've had and the roles you've performed, but try not to get angry about the bad decisions you believe you've made.

And don't wish that you could turn the clock back: if you do, you'll remain chained to your old life and you won't be able to move forwards as easily.

Accept things the way they are

This was definitely a challenge for me as I changed course. However, over time, by applying the principles I've described in this book, and by meeting people like Steve and listening to what they said to me, I started to accept that this was the way things were. I could only go *forwards*.

I didn't understand *why* I'd had this stroke that had turned my family's and my own life upside down, but the only sensible option was to try to *accept* it. And the more I did this – accepted that I could do nothing about what had happened in the past – the more I started to see other new opportunities opening up for me.

And now, seven years on, I can see the many positive outcomes that came out of the stroke. It gave me the chance to do new things – things I believed I'd never do, and which I feel make a real difference – to me, anyway. It has allowed me to take the experience I gained in my previous roles and to apply it to the new activities and new roles I'm now undertaking.

It also showed me what my priorities should be in life, and that some of the things I once believed were important actually aren't. In the main, my life is better now than it was before the stroke – the life in which I had a large salary and didn't have brain damage! My current mindset – the one I've tried to apply for a number of years now – is similar to Steve's: life goes forwards not backwards.

Some of the things that happen in your new life will be great, and you'll feel that everything is going to plan. Others, though, won't be so good. Sometimes you'll find yourself in challenging and difficult situations, and you'll start to question why you've changed direction. Or, if you've been forced into making a change, you'll question the *fairness* of it all: you can't understand *why* this is happening to you.

It's at these times that you must try to believe that the outcome will be positive. In the heat of the moment, you may not understand why certain things are happening to you, but try to foster and hold on to a belief that positive things *will* emerge from this – believe that, eventually, things will work out for the best. Wherever possible, try to accept that this is the way things are.

Forget about going back – it's impossible. And don't try to control every aspect of your life in the hope that you'll make it perfect – impossible again. Just accept things as they are and move forwards.

If you hold on to this belief, you'll naturally find ways of getting around the obstacles and difficulties you'll face. Try to remember that you're moving forwards – in the right direction and for the right reasons.

Acceptance means that, if you do find yourself looking back on your old life, it won't be with regret, sadness or bitterness, but with wisdom. You can draw on the experiences you've had to help drive you forwards.

So, as you move forwards, there will be reasons to change course, and reasons *not to.* There will also be obstacles in your path. Don't use these obstacles as *excuses* not to change course. Let me explain the difference between reasons and excuses with some help from Tim.

Chapter 8

PRINCIPLES

The difference between reasons and excuses

During the summer months, when the club welcomes thousands of visiting players, the golf course where I caddie gets incredibly busy. This often means that a round of golf can take up to five hours. Some players get very stressed about this and therefore don't enjoy the game as much as they might have done.

Others don't mind how long the round takes. They actually like the fact that they can take their time and savour the breathtaking views across to the sandy beach, the Firth of Forth and its many islands, and on to the hills beyond. It really is a stunning place to play golf.

Tim from South Carolina was definitely in this latter camp. He was playing golf on his own, which is unusual. The advantage of caddying for a solo player is that they very often want to talk, and Tim was no exception.

He was in Scotland for two weeks for three reasons. Number one was to visit his son, who was studying at Edinburgh University. Number two was that he'd always wanted to play golf in Scotland and this was a great excuse to finally do just that. And lastly, he'd just resigned from his job and was taking some time off to figure out what he could do next in his life. He was in the process of changing course.

When I apologized to Tim about the slowness of the round, he replied: 'I'd rather be playing golf slowly in Scotland than what I had to put up with in my job. The fact that I'm here is good enough for me. I don't care how long it takes – it's just amazing to be here.'

What a great attitude, I thought. Tim then told me a bit more about the things he'd 'put up with' at work, and why he was no longer a director of the US charity where he'd spent the previous 12 years. It turned out that, nine months earlier, a new CEO had been recruited to run the charity, and this man had very different ideas about how the charity should be run, and what it should be focusing on, from those of the previous CEO.

Tim and his new boss didn't hit it off. Tim didn't like how he was running the charity, and he started to become aware that none of his ideas on how things could be improved were being taken on board. He was also being asked to do things that he felt were at odds with his principles.

So, three weeks before the golf trip, he'd resigned and walked out of his office. 'I'd had enough,' he explained. 'It was time for me to move on and go work for an organization whose aims I believed in. I wanted to work for someone with the same principles and ideas as my own.'

'Push and pull' reasons

So far in the book, I've focused mainly on what I call the 'pull' reasons to change course. I've highlighted these many times: find a role that you'll love and which you believe in; one that gives you a feeling you are making a difference and uses your strengths for most of the time.

These reasons will 'pull' you along with expectation, and in the belief that you can do new and positive things and take on different roles in your life. But, as we set out to change course, these reasons are still in the future. They pull us along to change course with a promise that things will be much better than they are at the moment.

Tim reminded me that, as well as the 'pull' reasons, there are equally powerful 'push' reasons for change, and some of these are the ones he described to me.

Push reasons tend to exist in the 'now' and are related to what you are *currently* doing – your role, your job or your pastimes.

I call them push reasons because they literally propel you out of your existing situation.

Push reasons might include scenarios in which:

- You are doing things that you feel are against your principles.
- You feel your ideas and suggestions aren't being listened to.
- You believe that you aren't valued, or that what you do isn't regarded as important by those around you.
- You don't get regular praise for what you do.
- The people you spend most of your time with aren't what you'd call close friends.

These are situations that are pushing you away from what you'd like to be doing with your life, and they are giving you a huge feeling of dissatisfaction. Ultimately, push reasons can give you the power to say: 'Life has to be better than this. I must be able to do things that don't result in the negative emotions I currently have.' They push you to do something different, to change course.

I greatly admire people like Tim, who decide to change course because of a principle, because their voice isn't being heard, or because they feel they aren't valued. They might not have the 'pull' reasons for changing course completely worked out, but they're determined to move on from their current situation.

They have faith in their own abilities and talents, and in the people they trust. To me, they have real integrity.

'Hold on' reasons

If you have some of these push reasons in your life, don't ignore them. Combined with pull reasons, they can make a very strong foundation for changing course. If you haven't acted on your push and pull reasons yet, take some time to consider why.

Maybe it's because you think there's a third type of reason – one equally as powerful as push and pull. Your thinking may go like this:

> *Hold on, scary thoughts are jumping into my mind now. You talk about my push and pull reasons for changing course, and I can relate to some of these in my life, but what about the reasons not to do it?*
>
> *Reasons such as: I need to pay the mortgage; I'm planning to take my children on holiday this year; I want to buy a new car. I'll need money to do these things, so surely these are good reasons not to change course at the moment?*

There's another reason, too: if I do try to change course, I might fail. Or, even worse, people will laugh at me for trying. What about that? I might be humiliated. Surely this is a powerful reason not to go down that road?

And, actually, there's a really good argument for not changing course until the children are a bit older. I should wait until I have more time for it, and then maybe my partner can help me to do it better.

Surely all these reasons are just as valid as the push and pull reasons?

But these 'hold on' reasons are *not* valid: they are just *excuses*. Excuses that you give to yourself to explain why you are still in a job you hate doing – a job which gives you no sense of value, but hey, it pays for your two-week summer holiday.

Excuses for not finishing that business plan when you know the idea is a brilliant one, but implementing it runs the risk that someone will laugh at you. Excuses for not applying for that job you know you'd love doing because you tell yourself you're too old for it. Excuses for not using some of the money in your savings account to take that sabbatical – but at least you're getting a reasonable rate of interest.

These are the excuses – not the *reasons* – that are preventing you from doing things that would change your life positively and significantly. Every day, we can all find excuses like these. In fact, I think a better word than excuses is *obstacles*: obstacles that have the potential to stop us from doing the things we were built for.

There are three ways of dealing with obstacles: go around them, remove them or just go straight through them. In other words, ignore them, deal with them, or realize they aren't obstacles at all. But don't let them stop you changing course.

As both a CEO and a caddie, I've met a number of people like Tim, who were motivated to change course based on their push reasons. They probably all had mortgages to pay, children at the 'wrong' age or fears that people might ridicule them, but they *still* went ahead and changed course.

I've also met many people who had a dream of doing something new in their lives – something they felt would make a difference. Their current lives were fine, but they knew they were not built for what they were doing. They reached a tipping point where they just had to change course. They had positive reasons – push and pull ones – to do new things. And so they did it.

And lastly, I met people in a similar position to my own, who had been forced to change course because of a health scare. Once they'd recovered as much as was possible, they had enormous obstacles in their way – blindness, cognitive issues, physical limitations – but they still found ways to get round, go through or just ignore these obstacles. Which, in turn, allowed them to move forwards in a positive new direction.

So, if you are at that tipping point, and are thinking that you should *finally* change course, use your pull and push reasons to ensure that you actually *do it*. Don't use excuses as reasons not to do new things. Find ways to get around the obstacles that will be in your way, because there will *always* be a way round them.

Here's what the great Olympic swimmer Michael Phelps has to say about all this, in his book *No Limits: The Will to Succeed*:

> *'So many people along the way, whatever it is you aspire to do, will tell you it can't be done. But all it takes is imagination. You dream. You plan. You reach. There will be obstacles. There will be doubters. There will be mistakes.*
>
> *'But with hard work, with belief, with confidence, and trust in yourself and those around you, there are no limits.'*

That is how you get around obstacles and banish excuses. You look at your reasons for changing course – the things that have inspired you to consider a new path – and then you stick to the belief that what you're doing is the right thing for you. And then you just do it.

Chapter 9

NIKE IS RIGHT!

Just do it

When I caddie, the one thing that constantly amazes me is that some people will want to play a game of golf *regardless* of the weather. It might be raining heavily, freezing cold, blowing a gale, or a combination of all three, but they still want to play and, of course, take their caddie with them to share the experience!

Paul from Seattle was one of those golfers. As we stood at the 1st tee – in pouring rain and with a strong wind in our faces – he turned to me and declared: 'I didn't come to Scotland to sit in the clubhouse. Let's just do it and see what happens. It could be fun!'

At that moment, 'fun' wasn't a word that sprang readily to my mind. But funnily enough, it turned out to be a great round – despite the fact that I was soaking wet by the end of it – and that was because of Paul's 'just do it' attitude.

He would simply walk up to the ball with his selected club in his hand and quickly hit the shot – giving the impression that he wasn't really thinking about it. He was 'just doing it'. Every now and again he'd ask my advice, but not often. He was confident in his own ability.

I joked with Paul that, despite the terrible weather, with his attitude we'd be in the clubhouse in no time at all – with a whisky to warm us up. He laughed and said that he applied this attitude, this philosophy, to all areas of his life.

'That's how I make decisions and get things done,' he confessed. 'I prefer just going for it and seeing what happens. Sometimes I make mistakes but that's balanced out by the opportunities and the experiences I get. If I didn't have that attitude I'd never make decisions.'

The phrase 'just do it' has become famous as the slogan of the sports company Nike. It's one of those American terms that has percolated into the UK, and it embodies perfectly the mindset and attitude you'll need when changing course, whatever your reasons for doing so.

Don't let your circumstances control you

By just going for it, and replacing the fear of failure with the possibility of success, you understand that it's your choice, and yours alone, to act on the opportunities, the possibilities, the ideas, the plans, the dreams and the thoughts that you have. Only *you* can make the final decisions that'll make your changing course a success.

The great news is that, by having a 'just do it' mindset, the decisions you make today will shape the 'you' of tomorrow. You control those decisions. It's up to you – no-one else – to make a success of them.

In my time in business, I attended numerous seminars and conferences, and the events I got the most out of were those in which the main speakers were successful entrepreneurs. Through listening to or talking to these people, I came to the conclusion that one of the fundamental traits of a successful entrepreneur was this attitude of 'just doing it'.

These individuals obviously realized that if they'd allowed their circumstances or their environment to define who they were, they would probably have failed. It was *their* decisions that determined how successful they turned out to be, and they all communicated the fact that *they* alone were responsible for making a success of their lives – no-one else.

This was a mindset I'd had when I co-founded Company Net in 1996. Without it, and the support of the people around me, I'm certain that the business would have failed. Seventeen years later, the company is still thriving, led by another CEO and run by a brilliant management team who have that same 'just do it' mindset.

However, as I discovered, there can be a big challenge, or threat, in adopting and retaining this mindset. When you're changing direction it means, naturally, that you are moving into new situations and experiencing things that you haven't encountered before. You will, at times, be way out of your comfort zone.

One way of coping with this uncertainty is to *resist* some of these new things, or to *avoid* making decisions that you aren't comfortable with. You may become very worried that you'll fail, and 'just do it' becomes 'don't do it'. When you're thinking like this, the chances are that you're allowing your circumstances and your environment to dictate your decisions.

This is how I behaved in the early years after my stroke. I was way out of my comfort zone, and I started blaming the stroke – my new circumstances – for my lack of action. All the decisions I was making were governed by the stroke.

I was very scared of failing, and of what people would think of me. For example, I felt I couldn't communicate via e-mail because I might make lots of spelling and other mistakes. I couldn't call an old client for a meeting because I might lose my words. I wouldn't meet people in restaurants because it would be too noisy and I wouldn't be able to follow the conversation. The list was endless.

The stroke gave me these *excuses* for not doing new things or making meaningful decisions. In fact, the thought of doing new things *terrified* me initially. This was the complete opposite of the 'just do it' attitude I'd had when I co-founded Company Net.

But, slowly, I started to come to the conclusion that allowing my circumstances to dictate my actions and decisions was not a very smart way to live. I realized that I'd been letting my circumstances *control* me. And as long as that continued it would be very difficult to make the right decisions. 'Just going for it' wouldn't be an option.

I'd always find excuses *not* to try things, either consciously or subconsciously. Yes, there were times to hold back and take stock, but it should have been my decision to do this rather than the circumstances dictating the pace. How could it ever be possible to embark on anything new or exciting?

Now, not someday

With the help of some good and wise friends, I started to change my thinking. Looking back, there was no single event that suddenly sparked this change. It was a gradual thing. A few insights, conversations I had, books I read. Over time, I just came to *accept* that this was the way things were.

I finally understood that the only difference between Neil *CEO* and Neil *stroke survivor* was that the former understood that everything was his choice while the latter had allowed his circumstances to dictate everything.

So, my strategy was to get back to the CEO-thinking that had been so successful for me, and that's when things really started to move forwards in my life. My 'just do it' attitude returned, and I decided that my *circumstances* would no longer shape my future – my *decisions* would.

In *The 4-hour Work Week*, US author and entrepreneur Timothy Ferriss says:

> *'For all of the most important things, the timing always sucks. Waiting for a good time to quit your job? The stars will never align and the traffic lights of life will never all be green at the same time. The universe doesn't conspire against you, but it doesn't go out of its way to line up the pins either.*
>
> *'Conditions are never perfect. "Someday" is a disease that will take your dreams to the grave with you. Pro and con lists are just as bad. If it's important to you and you want to do it "eventually", just do it and correct course along the way.'*

This is the mindset that I have today, and it feels like a huge weight has been lifted off my shoulders. When decisions need to be made, or when opportunities arise, I just try to apply the 'just do it' attitude. I accept and understand that I'll come up against choices and decisions all the time, and that it's my responsibility to face up to them, deal with them and act on them.

In so doing, I accept that 'conditions are never perfect'. I know that I'll sometimes make mistakes or poor decisions. I'll feel embarrassed when I 'lose' words, or use the wrong ones, when talking to people. I'll make errors in e-mails. I'll constantly forget things: the names of people I've known for many years, important events, what I did last week!

I know that I'll still get incredibly tired and irritable if I try to do too much, and that I'll regularly find myself in new situations that would once have been normal, but which are now potentially very stressful for me.

But if I'd allowed these circumstances (or conditions) to dictate the pace as I changed course, I would have ground to a halt a long time ago, instead of moving forwards in my life. This doesn't mean that things are always pleasant and good, but it does mean that I can be in charge of the decisions I make. It's up to me. *I'm* in control, not my circumstances.

I'm more confident in making decisions now. In 'just doing it' I find that I'm far more productive, that I get involved in a whole range of new things and that I get a feeling of making a difference. Yes, I still make mistakes every day but, as Paul said, I just accept that this will happen and I move on.

So, as you change course, here's my advice to you:

Don't let your circumstances or your environment determine whether or not your new way forwards is a success. Don't let a fear of failure, or what other people may think about you, stop you from moving on.

Put these negative thoughts aside and ensure that only positive decisions and choices shape your path. This will lead you to things that you'll love doing, and which you feel will make a difference. If you are able to adopt this mindset you'll become like Paul, and I think that's a more productive and enjoyable way to live.

As you change course, new opportunities will present themselves to you all the time, and by 'just doing it' you'll find the right course will open up for you to follow.

However, when you're embracing this mindset, and the others outlined in this section of the book, there are a few things you need to be aware of – and guard against – because they can pull you off course. I call these 'traps', and I'll be telling you about these in the next section, beginning with the story of Michael, who showed me how important it is not to make money your main motivator.

PART 3

CHANGING COURSE TRAPS

Chapter 10

TWO IN TEN

Don't focus solely on money

In my opinion, Michael from Cape Town should be awarded a Nobel Prize for common sense.

Michael was a venture capitalist – and from what I gathered during our conversation, he was a very good one. He'd flown to Scotland in his private jet with eight friends. No rushing to the airport to catch a flight for him: he leaves when he wants to!

He was also an excellent communicator. We chatted a lot, and he told me about some of the companies he'd invested in over the years. He'd made a lot of money from some of them, but with others, he'd lost a lot. I asked him about the criteria he'd apply to making an investment and he told me that however careful he was with his investments, he still expected only two in ten of them to be successful.

Only two! So eight would fail and he'd lose all his money. I remarked that those two investments had to be *very* successful. 'Yes,' he agreed with a smile. He then shared a fascinating insight with me. In his view, the 'two in ten' ratio can be applied to other areas in life – namely, happiness and money.

'Please explain,' I urged him (as I thought about his private jet that could fly eight people directly from South Africa to Scotland).

Michael explained that he'd worked in finance since leaving university – initially for an investment bank and then as a venture capitalist before going on to establish his own venture capitalist firm. A lot of his friends were also involved in the area of 'making money' – they worked as investment bankers, venture capitalists, bond traders, stockbrokers and so on.

Of all the people Michael knew with 'money-related' jobs, only two out of ten were what he'd call genuinely contented and happy. The rest were, well, unhappy. They were divorced or in failing marriages; and they were stressed, selfish, angry, unfit, alcoholics... Money – Michael insisted – and making it, had made them miserable.

Now that you are thinking of heading in a new direction (or perhaps you've already done so), it's well worth looking at what you want from a new role, career or job, and what sacrifices you're prepared to make.

But whatever you decide to do, be sure that making a lot of money isn't your main motivator. To reinforce this point, here's a story that Michael shared with me:

An American businessman was standing on the pier in a village on the coast of Mexico when a small boat with just one fisherman docked. Inside his boat were several large yellowfin tuna.

The American complimented the fisherman on the quality of his fish and asked him how long it took to catch them.

'Only a little while,' the Mexican replied.

The American then asked the man why he didn't stay out longer and catch more fish. The Mexican said that he caught enough to meet his family's needs.

'But what do you do with the rest of your time?' the American asked.

'I sleep late, fish a little, play with my children, take a siesta with my wife, Maria. Each evening I stroll into the village, where I sip wine and play guitar with my amigos. I have a full and busy life, señor.'

The American scoffed at this: 'I'm a Harvard MBA and I could help you,' he said. 'You should spend more time fishing, and with the proceeds, buy a bigger boat.

With the proceeds from the bigger boat, you could buy several boats. Eventually, you'd have a fleet of fishing boats, and instead of selling your catch to a middleman you'd sell it directly to the processor.

'Then you could open your own cannery. You'd control the product, processing and distribution. You'd need to leave this small fishing village and move to Mexico City, then on to Los Angeles, and, eventually, to New York City, where you'd run your expanding enterprise.'

'But señor, how long would all this take?' the fisherman asked.

'Fifteen, maybe 20 years,' the American replied.

'But what then, señor?'

The American laughed and said: 'That's the best part. When the time is right, you would announce an IPO and sell your company stock to the public. You'd become very rich. You'd make millions!'

'Then what, señor?'

'Then you'd retire. Move to a small fishing village on the coast, where you'd sleep late, fish a little, play with your grandchildren, take a siesta with your wife. In the evening you could stroll to the village, sip wine and play guitar with your amigos.'

Michael told this story to some of his friends and peers – those whose world is based around making money. In different ways, they'd all commented that, in hindsight, they'd known even before they were successful what was *really* important in life.

Focusing on money, making it their number one priority, had taken them away from that, and had resulted in many of them leading unhappy lives. These were people who, in the main, earned seriously big salaries. They'd been driven by money to reach the point where they'd finally have the things that would make them happy and contented. But they never got there.

The irony is that they were probably there at the very start of their careers, when they had very little. Just ask that Mexican fisherman what's important in life!

So, this is the warning I want to highlight. Whatever you do, and whatever decisions you make as you change course, don't do it simply because you want to earn a lot of money. That will lead you into Michael's 'two in ten' world.

Of course, the chances are that you'll still need to earn money – and the only way to do that is by doing a new job, role or career. But don't fall into the trap of looking at the salary *before* you work out whether you'll *love* doing whatever you've chosen.

This will be very difficult for you, but take your time and put doing a job or a role that you feel *makes a difference* at the top of your list. Examine all the aspects of a particular role or job you think you'll enjoy doing and *then* look at the salary.

As the philosopher, writer and speaker Alan Watts said:

> *'If you say that getting the money is the most important thing, you will spend your life completely wasting your time. You'll be doing things you don't like doing in order to go on living – that is to go on doing things you don't like doing. Which is stupid!*
>
> *'Better to have a short life that is full of what you like doing than a long life spent in a miserable way.'*

For those of you who are in the fortunate position of being able to survive without a salary for a while, you now have a great opportunity – you can take your time finding out what you'll love doing. There's no excuse not to do the things that'll fill you with purpose and passion.

But if you are concerned about paying next month's mortgage, it's best to create some 'personal commitments' around changing course. This, then, is commitment number one:

Whatever I do, I will try to do something I will love – not for money, not for status, but just because it feels natural to do it, and I'm using my talents.

The way to apply this rule, and to make sure that you keep to it, is to understand what you're trying to achieve in the *long term* – really, the 'ultimate goal' of whatever it is you're doing. What do you want your *legacy* to be? What is the 'dent in the universe' you are trying to achieve?

Be driven by your personal vision

As you change direction, you'll need a *personal vision* of where you eventually want to be. This book offers ideas and suggestions as you begin this journey, but to stay on the right path – heading towards something you are passionate about, which provides you with purpose and uses your talents for most of the time – you'll need to know *where* you are going.

Here's a useful exercise for finding your personal vision:

Imagine that it's ten years on from today, and you've been invited to a party to celebrate the first decade of your new life. The key people in your world are there – your family, your friends and close colleagues. Each of them has been asked to speak about you for five minutes, outlining what you've achieved over the past ten years.

How would you want them to describe your life, your character, your mindset, since you changed course?

Your answers to this will be your personal vision, your overall goal, your quest. This vision is *what you want to achieve*. This is the 'dent in the universe' you're trying to make. It's what you're aiming *to be,* and the *legacy* you want to leave. It's not how much money you earn.

Your personal vision will act as your 'sat nav' and keep you on the right path – which means you'll look at your vision before you look at the salary.

When I do this exercise, I imagine what one of my closest friends will say about me. It's a great motivator when I have writer's block, or when I'm tempted to do things which, on paper, might earn me more money, but give me little personal satisfaction:

> *'Over the last ten years Neil has written three books which have had a positive impact on people's lives. His* Changing Course *series has helped thousands of individuals, groups and companies.'*

That, to me, is my little dent in the universe, and it keeps me writing!

So, the next time you have to make a decision about a potential new role or opportunity, go back to your personal vision of what you want to achieve and be, and see if it can help you. If you allow yourself to be guided by your vision, and what you wish your legacy to be, you may earn less than you used to, or less than what your friends earn, but you'll be more contented, more balanced and less stressed.

Now, one outcome of doing things that give you purpose and passion might well be that you earn a very good living, or even become wealthy. And that's great. But whatever you do, don't look to find ways of getting wealthy *first,* and then search for passion and purpose in the roles you do. It just won't work out well.

You could say that Michael was one of the lucky ones. He earned a lot of money, was using his talents and loved what he did. But let's not kid ourselves. He was the exception to the 'two in ten' rule. And you really don't want to fall into that trap.

Another trap you need to be aware of when changing course is the need to stick to reality. To illustrate this, let me tell you about Liz.

Chapter 11

CON AIR

Stick to reality

When you watch a Hollywood action film, how often do you know someone who has one of the occupations portrayed in it? Pretty rarely, I'd guess.

For example, in many movies the lead character is a CIA agent, and to my sure and certain knowledge (I think!) not one of my friends or acquaintances is a CIA employee. And there are plenty of films in which the 'hero' is a murder detective. Number of those in my address book? Zero.

In general, then, I'd guess that the people you know are similar to the people I know, and their occupations are not usually seen in action movies. Most of the people I caddie for are like this, too. But Liz from Denver, well, her occupation was a bit different from the rest.

Have you seen the action movie *Con Air*, starring Nicolas Cage? As the film starts, a group of convicts are being transferred to a new prison via a prisoner transport plane. Without wanting to ruin the film for you if you haven't seen it, some of the prisoners take control of the plane with the idea of escaping, and Cage (a prisoner who is being released) tries to stop them. (I think I've just ruined it!)

I really like this movie, so when Liz told me what her occupation was, it made me smile. 'I'm a pilot, but not a commercial pilot,' she said. 'I work for the Justice Prisoner and Alien Transportation system.'

'Wow!' I exclaimed. 'I knew the American government had caught aliens – Area 51 and all that!'

Liz laughed and told me that the government agency she works for is actually known as Con Air. 'We are the agency charged with the transportation of prisoners between prisons, detainee centres, courthouses and other locations,' she explained. Her primary role was flying prisoners across the USA.

'So, at long last, I've met someone whose job comes straight out of an action film,' I remarked. Liz smiled. 'Yes, it probably does sound exciting and adventurous,' she admitted, 'but trust me, it isn't. Don't believe what you see in the movies! What I do is actually pretty boring. The image portrayed is completely different from the reality.'

Find your true path

Changing course can be a very exciting new development in your life – a chance to try something you thought you'd never get the opportunity to do. But there's always a possibility that you'll choose the wrong path, or do something for the 'wrong' reasons.

One of those wrong reasons is what I call the Perfect Lifestyle Syndrome. I think all of us have succumbed to this at some point in our lives. In fact, for a lot of people – and I include myself here – it's almost a yearly occurrence, especially in autumn and winter, when a certain type of programme starts to appear on TV.

The signs of the syndrome play out like this. You watch one of those 'lifestyle' programmes featuring a couple in their early thirties called Ben and Katie who have decided to leave their jobs and home in the city and move to Tuscany in Italy. Out there, they've bought a 300-year-old farmhouse (which none of the locals will live in) and they're renovating it.

Their plan is to rent part of the farmhouse to paying guests, starting the following summer. They have just six months to make it work or they'll run out of money.

As the show progresses, it becomes obvious that Ben and Katie don't have much experience of building work, as they get into more and more trouble with the house renovation. We also discover that Katie can only speak a little Italian, while Ben speaks none. Therefore, Katie has to deal with all the paperwork and Italian bureaucracy – and again, this doesn't go well. Finally, the whole project starts to go over budget and this puts a strain on the couple's relationship.

However, there are some clear upsides to Ben and Katie's situation. The location of their farmhouse is stunning, the Tuscan countryside is breathtaking, the help they get from their neighbours is wonderful and so, together with lots of al fresco wining and dining, these things compensate for the difficulties.

In fact, it all seems rather idyllic. Even though, week in, week out, they have problems, they seem to be very happy with the decision they've made. Finally, with a day to spare, part of the farmhouse is eventually ready for rental and paying guests arrive. The last scene of the show sees Ben and Katie sitting on the grass in front of the farmhouse, sipping wine as the sun sets behind them.

As you are watching this, you start to question your own life. You start to think that trying something similar to what Ben and Katie are doing will make you happy. You see a new future, a new course, emerging.

These aspirational shows are on TV every week – all of them presenting you with the dream of *your* perfect life. You become convinced that *you'd* love to do what the people in the show are doing. In your mind (or perhaps even in reality), you decide that you need to change course in your life and open that restaurant, or move to France to run a hotel, or take your whole family sailing around the world

It becomes your goal: *this* is what will make you happy and give you the perfect lifestyle. But there's one thing to be aware of:

You need to be sure that the 'perfect lifestyle' in your mind is not completely different from reality.

If you follow that TV or Hollywood dream without a 'reality check', there's a good chance that you'll find yourself in a worse situation than if you hadn't changed course at all.

In his book *Handbook For The Soul,* Richard Carlson has this to say about following someone else's dream:

> *'Find your true path. It's so easy to become someone we don't want to be, without even realizing it's happening. We are created by the choices we make every day. And if we take action in order to please some authority figure, we'll suddenly wake up down the road and say, "This isn't me. I never wanted to be this person".'*

Substitute the words 'in order to please some authority figure' for 'follow a TV chef, property expert or explorer', and you get my warning. In the last chapter I talked about creating some personal commitments around changing course – to help avoid some of the traps you might fall into. Well, here's the second one:

I won't let myself be brainwashed into doing something that I wasn't meant to, just because it looks and sounds great on TV, in a movie or in a book.

Be the person who goes where their natural talents and strengths take them. Be the person who feels they are making a difference. Be the person who jumps out of bed and loves what they do because it's the most natural thing for them, and because it's what they've wanted to do for so long.

Now, funnily enough, doing just that could result in you undertaking something that *is* featured in one of these TV shows. That's great: the TV companies may be knocking on your door to film you doing it! But, whatever you do, do it because you want a feeling of making a difference rather than following an *image* of a life that's completely different from the *reality* of living it.

If you remember this, whether you're running a guest house in Tuscany, working for a bank in the city, staying at home to look after your children, or flying a plane full of convicts, you'll be on the right course. *And you will know it.*

Chapter 12

PREDICTIVE TEXTING

Don't make assumptions

It never ceases to amaze me how quickly children pick up new technology. My kids seem to know instinctively how to use or play a new gadget, game, app or computer as soon it appears in our house. Although I'm much slower at learning how to use it, I still love new technology.

However, there's one technology that my kids love and seem to have mastered, and which I absolutely loathe (and can never control), and that's predictive texting.

I'd like to think that I'm generally a patient man, but if someone (usually one of my children) has switched my phone to predictive text mode, I can lose my temper pretty quickly. In my humble opinion, the main problem with predictive texting is that it's rubbish at predicting. It automatically inserts what's usually the wrong word, and if you aren't very careful, you end up sending a text message that makes no sense.

After five years of caddying, I've come to the following conclusion: like predictive texting, I'm rubbish at predicting what my round of golf as a caddie will be like.

You see, I've no idea who I'm going to caddie for until I see the person on the practice green. I don't get to meet them until the 1st tee. And it's in between those stages that I start to make assumptions about how the person will be as a golfer. Will they be relaxed, will they be fun to be around, and will they be chatty?

These predictions are based on my experience of caddying for many different kinds of people, and I have to admit that the vast majority of these predictions have been completely wrong. Most people are *completely* different from what I expect them to be. One great example of this was Mayu from Japan.

Before I'd even been introduced to Mayu, I'd made a prediction about her. It went something like this: she'd be a poor golfer, have a high handicap, would be slow in her play, and wouldn't communicate with me very much. It was a very windy day and in my mind I predicted that she'd really struggle. I thought that she'd get very frustrated and wouldn't enjoy her experience, and therefore my tip would be rubbish!

I wasn't looking forward what I thought was going to be a very long round.

But how wrong was my prediction! Mayu was one of the most delightful people I've ever caddied for, and she was a brilliant golfer. What was even more astounding for me was her age (she volunteered the information – I didn't ask!). I'd guessed that she was in her early forties, but it turned out she was 68. She put her youthful looks down to eating a lot of fish!

Mayu stood no taller than 1.5 metres (5 feet), but she could hit the ball for miles – straight every time. And she was very generous when it came to tipping! I had a great round with her, and after that wonderful experience I decided I would try to stop predicting. Instead, I'd just wait and see what people turned out to be like.

Look only at the facts

This is also a very good philosophy to keep in the front of your mind when you are changing course: *don't try to predict how things will turn out.* There's a good chance that you'll be wrong, so you will just waste time and energy and make yourself more anxious about the outcome. Predicting may even prevent you from making the decisions you need to make, and it could even push you into making the *wrong* decisions.

I've mentioned before that taking a new direction in life will cause a significant level of uncertainty. You're at the start of a new road, and that means lots of new experiences. There'll be big decisions to make for which there'll be no obvious answers. It's natural, therefore, to want a sense of control.

You'll be looking for certainty, and because of that you'll make predictions and assumptions about what might happen. Your thinking may go something like this:

If I can predict what'll happen, it will give me a better chance to control things. And if I can control things, I can be more certain about the decisions I'm making. If I can predict accurately, I'll make good decisions. Therefore, it's logical for me to try to predict outcomes and make assumptions.

The trouble is, we aren't very good at predicting when we don't have all the facts. And for most of the decisions we make, we generally *don't* have *all* the facts. So we start making assumptions and predictions to fill in the gaps, and this is a dangerous path to be on.

I love the following (allegedly) true story of a 1995 radio conversation between a US Navy aircraft carrier (USS *Abraham Lincoln*) and Canadian authorities off the coast of Newfoundland, as it illustrates this point very well.

Canadians: Please divert your course 15 degrees to the south to avoid collision.

Americans: Recommend you divert your course 15 degrees to the north to avoid collision.

Canadians: Negative. You will have to divert your course 15 degrees to the south to avoid collision.

Americans: This is the captain of a US Navy ship. I say again: divert your course.

Canadians: No, I say again, you divert your course.

Americans: This is the aircraft carrier USS Abraham Lincoln, the second largest ship in the United States Atlantic fleet. We are accompanied by three destroyers, three cruisers and numerous support vessels. I demand that you change your course 15 degrees north. I say again, that's one five degrees north – or counter-measures will be undertaken to ensure the safety of this ship.

Canadians: This is a lighthouse. Your call.

The lesson from this story is that even when you think you're in a strong position, if you don't have all the facts you can still get it wrong.

We are quick to assume things. We *think* we know how things will turn out. We start looking at one fact about a situation and then, in an attempt to get to a position of certainty, we begin to make predictions and assumptions about what might happen. Our thinking can then start to spiral out of control.

It's natural to want to make assumptions about the future, and to attempt to predict how things might turn out. This is dangerous, though, because your assumptions are likely to be based on opinion and hope, rather than 100% fact.

What's worse is that, when we think we've put in methods of thinking that'll provide us with certainty, life has a funny way of surprising us. During my time as a CEO, one event showed me that even though I believed I could predict what would happen, in reality I could not.

The unforeseeable scenario

In 2006, I attended a conference in London at the Royal Albert Hall. This is a wonderful building, right next to Hyde Park where the Princess Diana Memorial Fountain is situated. As the conference had been very intense, and I had a lot on my mind, I decided to go for a walk in the park to think.

Company Net had recently received a buyout offer from an American company, and our board was due to meet the next day to make a final decision on whether or not to accept the offer. I was personally and professionally undecided on whether I would vote to sell the company.

So, I sat in the park and wrote down what I saw as the pros and cons of selling. I also compiled a list of the potential scenarios that might or might not occur in each of those pros and cons. This is the 'what if' method of predicting.

My list contained items such as, 'American company buys us for £x and I get invited onto their board'; 'Our board rejects the offer but the business climate changes, profits dwindle, and the value of our shares is halved within a year'; 'The board accepts the offer and I receive a cash offer for my shares and leave'. In total, I wrote a list of 12 potential scenarios.

In the end, I decided not to sell my shares and voted against selling the company. And that's what the majority of my board agreed to do. My decision was based on my prediction that my staying as CEO in the medium term offered the best prospects for the shareholders, the staff and myself.

I predicted that the shareholders would receive a better deal in one or two years' time if I could grow the company significantly over that period. I was *certain* that this was a good prediction. However, three months after I made that list and came to my decision, I had the stroke. Not one of my 12 scenarios predicted that particular outcome.

Seven years on, I still have that piece of paper with my list of scenarios. It helps to remind me that, however good I think I am at predicting, things can actually turn out in the most surprising and unexpected ways!

I'm not saying that you shouldn't have visions, dreams or goals, and that you shouldn't plan as you are changing course

– I think those things are critical if you want to be successful. But making predictions and assumptions based on a feeling, or half a story, or an opinion, where you don't have up-to-date facts is probably a waste of your time and your energy.

So, here's the third personal commitment to make when changing course:

I will try not to make predictions or assumptions about what might or might not happen in the future. The best solution is, wherever possible, to live in the moment and deal with things when they actually happen.

Base your decisions about the numerous opportunities that will come you way on the *facts* alone. Just stick with the principles, ideas and insights outlined in this book, and take each day as it comes.

In my case, I know that the choice is always mine. Either I can make lots of assumptions and try to predict the future, or I can just accept things as they currently are – looking at the facts and coping with different situations as and when they arise.

I accept now that some outcomes will be good, others not so good. Some things will take time to happen while others will be far quicker.

My experience with Mayu showed me that trying to predict the future is a fruitless exercise. It's far better to live in the here and now and look only at the facts. When I do this, I find that I'm far less stressed and enjoy my life more. Until, of course, I have to deal with predictive texting on my phone!

Chapter 13

STEPPING STONES

Don't dwell on what you used to do

'I feel completely invisible now,' said Mitch from Texas as we walked up the 2nd fairway. I knew exactly what he meant. Mitch used to be the CEO of a large construction company in the USA, and the key words here are 'used to'.

Mitch had worked at the company for 25 years, rising to be the CEO ten years previously. Then, in 2008, his life changed completely.

Driving to work on a regular Tuesday morning, he stopped at some traffic lights. But the driver behind him didn't stop, and drove straight into the back of Mitch's car. Even though Mitch was wearing a seat belt, the impact of the crash was significant. He suffered a serious head injury and was in hospital for weeks.

Mitch recovered well physically, but cognitively he had major complications. Part of his brain was permanently damaged – the bit that deals with memory and attention. And he felt incredibly tired most of the time.

After six months of recovery, Mitch tried to return to his job as a CEO. But he just *couldn't* do it. He couldn't concentrate in meetings; his ability to remember facts was gone; and he couldn't do more than one thing at a time. He also had to have a nap during the day. Even though his company was initially supportive, the board eventually decided that he should resign.

Mitch told me all this as we played the first few holes, and I could empathize completely with what he was going through. He was the first person I'd met – not only through caddying, but in other areas of my life – who'd described perfectly the many problems I'd experienced following my stroke.

That, I think, is why Mitch opened up to me so much about how he was feeling. The symptoms he described, his emotions and some of the thoughts he had to live with – were exactly the same as mine had been.

However, after caddying for Mitch for well over four hours, I discovered that there was a fundamental difference between us on how we were coping with changing course. He seemed depressed, and wished he could turn the clock back to the time before his car crash.

It seemed to me that he was really struggling with the loss of his status – of now being an ex-CEO. That is why he'd used those words, 'I feel invisible now'. As well as having an air of depression about him, Mitch came across as being angry and very stressed. Altogether, he was finding it really difficult to accept his new life.

You can't turn the clock back

I, on the other hand, was at the stage of accepting my new life. I was starting to see other opportunities opening up: ones that I could potentially get involved in. But it hadn't always been like that. For a while, and we are talking about a year or so after the stroke, I'd felt just like Mitch did.

You see, I had loved being a CEO. And to be brutally honest, I'd also loved the 'badge' that came with it. The role made me feel important. Valued. It fuelled my ego. The meetings I led, the pitches we tackled, the buzz of winning new business, the conferences I attended and spoke at, the business trips, the long lunches with clients, the corporate hospitality. I had loved it all.

Before the stroke, a typical week would involve presenting to senior executives in the boardroom of a large company, running planning sessions with my leadership team, approving financial budgets and estimates for projects, interviewing potential staff and working on new marketing strategies.

The week following the stroke, I could barely *speak*. I didn't understand what people were saying to me. I was incredibly tired, and I was an emotional mess.

And that's why I could relate to Mitch's situation. I understood what he meant by the word 'invisible'. My role as a CEO had gone, and in some ways that had defined who I was. Once it was taken away, I felt invisible too, for a long while.

So, here's something that you, too, must watch out for on your journey:

When you embark on something new, a lot of the things that define you to others will go. The 'badge' of who you are disappears. In some ways, you'll feel as if you're back at the beginning.

Now, you might be thinking that surely the whole point of this book is to help you change course and start again – and that the core message is to follow your dream and take on things you're passionate about. You want to *remove* the old badge and do something completely new in your life, right?

Of course, you're right about the book's message. It's important though, to be aware that, even though you might be desperate to change course, there will undoubtedly be times when you miss your old life, especially when things start to get tough or challenging (as they inevitably will).

And, as Mitch found, it's even more difficult if you're in the situation of being *forced* to change course. Then, missing your old role, the badge that said who you are, can be very hard to cope with.

You'll probably start to realize that what you once did for a living, or the role you once occupied, defined *who* you were: a mother of young children, a doctor, an IT director, a marketing manager, whatever. And now it has gone. The teenage children have left home, you've been forced to retire, your job has been made redundant, your business is put into administration...

In the Western world, we largely define people by what they do for a living. Just think back to the last time you were at a party or some other social gathering and you met someone for the first time. I bet that within a few sentences of being introduced to them, the conversation got around to roles or what you do for a living.

When you change course, especially at the start of the process, you'll find that removing your badge – that identifier of who you are – can be a big blow to your ego. You might even start to feel a bit worthless or, as Mitch described it, 'invisible'.

This is one of the big challenges you'll have to face – how to cope with your feelings when you lose your previous life and the status that went with it. And trust me, at some point you *will* miss them.

For some of you, these feelings might not last long, and you may be able to let go of your old life quite easily. However, for others, and I include myself here, these feelings and thoughts can linger for a long while. You may start to have regrets, or become angry. It's possible that you'll even start to think that changing course wasn't such a great idea after all.

At this point, you just need to *accept* that it'll take time to adjust to your new life. There's no easy solution to all of this. You just need to understand that a part of you has gone. You can grieve for it. You can get sad about it. You can even get angry about it. *But don't dwell on it.*

Don't waste time and energy wishing you could turn the clock back, because you can't. If you try to do that, the chances are that it'll hold you back, and you won't come close to fulfilling your potential. Your old life will not return, so your only option is to move forwards.

It was when I *really* understood all of this that new and exciting things started to happen again in my life. It was when I let go of wishing I could do my old job again that changing course became an exciting adventure with so many opportunities.

Getting past the rocks in the road

And this is certainly how you should see changing course – as an adventure, an opportunity to do new things. By all means look back and think about what you used to do and be, because that's where you'll draw some of the wisdom you'll need to make the right decisions going forwards.

As the German philosopher Friedrich Nietzsche said:

> *'There will always be rocks in the road ahead of us. They will be stumbling blocks or stepping stones: it all depends on how you use them.'*

Looking back at your old life is an *enabler* that will allow you to do new things. And this brings us to personal commitment number four:

I will view the role I once had as a stepping stone that will get me closer to doing the things I really want to do (even though I might not know what they are yet!)

You might think that you had the perfect job and then you were forced to change course. As a result, you may believe that nothing will be as good as it used to be. I certainly used to think that. My stroke was my stumbling block. It gave me *excuses* not to do new things, and it provided me with *reasons* to get angry or depressed.

But, over time, I started to view my stroke as the *catalyst* to do new things: to look for new opportunities. It has led me to a completely different life, one that is, in many ways, better than the one I had before.

You may have chosen to change course, or you may have been forced into it, but then found 'rocks' in the way. Whatever your starting point, and however big you imagine these rocks are, try to find ways of seeing them as stepping stones towards new opportunities. You might just be pleasantly surprised where these stepping stones will take you, if you just give it time.

Finally, there's another challenge you need to be aware of. As well as focusing on your *strengths*, you need to know how to manage your *limitations* (or weaknesses), and to avoid the trap of thinking you can or should do everything. To see how this works, let me introduce you to Bob.

Chapter 14

THE PHILOSOPHY OF JACK

Manage your limitations

One of the great joys of caddying is getting to meet a wide range of golfers. They all have different abilities: some are great players with very low handicaps; others are beginners, and for them, getting one par in the round is a huge achievement.

However, regardless of whether a player has a low or a high handicap, there's one big thing that separates them into two distinct groups – and that's whether they know their *limitations* as golfers. Those who do, usually have an enjoyable round. Those who don't, tend to get stressed and frustrated.

Bob from Texas knew *his* limitations. Throughout the whole round, he only took on the shots he *knew* he could make. For example, rather than trying to hit a very difficult 220-yard shot from the rough to the green, he'd be patient and hit it in two shots, ensuring that he'd still get to the green. He knew what his limitations were and played his round accordingly.

As we walked up to the 14th hole, I told Bob that a lot of people I caddie for think they are Tiger Woods and try to hit shots that are well-nigh impossible for them. Then they get angry with themselves – and with their caddie!

'I was once one of those golfers,' Bob confessed. 'I'd try to hit shots that were way above my ability, and I'd get stressed and not enjoy the round. However, over the last ten years or so, I've changed my philosophy to one that says I need to understand and accept what my limitations are. Then I use strategies to compensate for those limitations. This allows me to focus on what I *am* good at.

'I do this in golf, in my business; in fact, in all areas of my life,' he went on. 'And here's a thing – since I applied that philosophy, my business has really grown. And golf has become far more enjoyable.'

Bob was the CEO of a large Kansas-based printing company that he'd founded in the late 1990s. For the first seven years of its existence, Bob's company stayed relatively small, and during that time he felt he should be involved in all aspects of the business. He was, after all, the CEO. But then, in mid-2000, he had a health scare.

At a yearly medical checkup, his doctor informed him that his blood pressure was so high there was a strong possibility that he'd have a heart attack. He was warned that he needed to calm down, cut back on the hours he was working and work 'smarter', both at the office and in his personal life.

'And you know,' Bob said, 'it's funny how things happen.' The week after the doctor's visit he happened to tune in to a documentary that included an interview with the great golfer, Jack Nicklaus.

Jack's message, Bob said, was very simple but incredibly powerful, and it went something similar to this:

> *'Golf is a game where you have to understand yourself: you have to understand what your own abilities are, and you have to play within them. If you get outside that, that's when you get beat.'*

Jack's philosophy had a big effect on Bob, and he decided to apply it to his own life. Up to that point in his career, he'd felt that he'd had to be good at everything, or at least give the impression that he was. Looking back, he could see how ineffective that was. And, more importantly, how stressful it was and how bad for his health. It was no surprise that he had high blood pressure.

So, after that wake-up call, Bob started to implement new ways of working in his business. He employed a new leadership team – one made up of people with complementary strengths, knowledge and skills from his own. This allowed him to focus on the things *he* was really good at – sales and marketing.

And the business started to flourish. Four years later, he was running one of the biggest printing companies in the Midwest of the USA.

Stay within your comfort zone

Changing course could be a really positive thing for you – as it was for me. Early in the book, I highlighted how important it is to do something that you'll love, and which will see you making the most of your talents.

I know you're probably thinking that this philosophy – just focus on your strengths and things will work out fine – is *way* too simple. And you're right! It *will* be impossible to do this *all* of the time, because every day you'll be in situations in which you'll be asked, or forced, to do things outside your core strengths. Or you'll have to operate in areas in which you are weak or have limitations.

So, in light of this, here is the fifth and final personal commitment:

I must learn to manage my limitations, my weaknesses, because when I achieve that it will leave me with more time to capitalize on my strengths.

As Jack Nicklaus said, you have to 'understand what your own abilities are and play within them'. Once you start moving out of your comfort zone – spending too much time doing things that *don't* involve your core talents – you're likely to 'get beat', and your changing course journey will not be as successful. Don't believe you can do everything well!

You should focus on what you are good at doing, and if possible, get help and support with the other things. I'm certainly *not* suggesting that you stop having dreams and ambitions to do something new – this book is all about doing just that – but the key is *how* you do that new thing.

For me, Marcus Buckingham sums this up perfectly in his book *The Truth About You: Your Secret To Success*, in which he says:

> *'You grow most in your areas of greatest strength. It sounds odd, but you will improve the most, be the most creative, be the most inquisitive, and bounce back the fastest in those areas where you have already shown some natural advantage over everyone else – your strengths.*
>
> *'This doesn't mean you should ignore your weaknesses. It just means you'll grow most where you're already strong.'*

So, if you want to make your new direction in life a success, you'll need to do the following:

- Understand and manage your limitations (weaknesses). (The next chapter focuses on a method that will help you to identify these.)

- Try to minimize the amount of time you spend on them.

- Spend most of your time focusing on the things you are naturally *good* at, while managing those areas in which you aren't so adept.

How do you split your time? Well, a good rule of thumb is to ask yourself this fundamental question: 'Do I feel that I have the opportunity to do what I do best every day, for most of the time – at work, at home and in all areas of my life?'

Once you can answer that question with a 'yes', you'll find you are more productive, and much happier. And one of the ways to help you get a 'yes' answer every day is to learn to manage your limitations.

Create a 'rule book'

When I applied this rule as CEO of Company Net, I found I could focus on the things I was good at, and either delegate or work with someone who had the strengths I didn't possess. I was managing my limitations, and as a result the company became more productive and successful.

This was relatively easy, as I had a large team working for me; it's far more difficult to achieve if you're going it alone. The principle of doing what you're good at, and managing your limitations, still applies, though.

For me, one of the lessons that came out of my stroke was the reinforcement of this principle. The stroke really *magnified* my limitations, and I was simply unable to do some of the things I'd done before. If I tried, I would get 'beat' – and quickly! So I was determined to do the things I *could* do well every day, and to manage my weaknesses and limitations as much as possible.

Once I started to do this, I found I became less frustrated and more productive, and I started taking some new directions in my life. But, in developing those new things, I'm still spending most of my time using my core strengths – such as being proactive and having empathy – and complementing these by seeking help or delegating my areas of weakness.

In addition, to help me manage my limitations, I've put together a 'rule book in my mind' for coping in situations where I know I'll have difficulties. For example, one of those situations would be attending meetings in a restaurant or a café, as I tend to struggle in busy or noisy environments. To counter this limitation, I arrive at the meeting 15 minutes early and locate the quietest table available. That's one rule.

Another is ensuring that I don't set up too many meetings on any given day, because I know that I'll become incredibly tired, and consequently unproductive, the following day. Writing this book presented many new challenges, too, but I made it a rule to draft the chapters and then ask a good friend and my wife to check the text and edit where necessary.

So, try to focus on your strengths and develop your own changing course 'rule book' on how to manage your limitations and weaknesses. Don't be scared to ask for help or support from others (more about this later on in the book).

In doing these things, you'll be able to answer 'yes' to the question, 'Do I feel that I have the opportunity to do what I do best every day, for most of the time?' A successful strategy for managing everything around this issue will make your changing course journey more enjoyable, rewarding and fulfilling.

So, we've looked at the traps of changing course, and the personal commitments you can make to avoid falling into them. Now, the new discoveries…

PART 4

CHANGING COURSE DISCOVERIES

Chapter 15

THE JOHARI HOUSE

Identify your blind self

Every now and again, I get the opportunity to caddie for someone who has a different type of job – one that I've never even heard of. Helen from Minneapolis was one such person. She told me that she was a business psychologist, and the way I looked at her prompted her to say, 'You have no idea what that is, do you?'

I had to admit that I didn't, but that I was intrigued.

It turned out that Helen, actually Dr Helen, had studied psychology at university, where she'd gained a PhD and had then gone on to do an MBA at Harvard University. Her focus there, both academically and now in business, was studying CEOs and what makes them successful. Or not!

For the previous ten years, Helen had been running a consultancy, working with companies in the USA to help their

CEOs and senior directors become more effective. She did this by using traditional psychology methods, supplemented by her extensive business qualifications and experience. So Dr Helen was a business psychologist.

As we walked down to the 7th hole, I asked Helen whether there was one thing, more than any other, which could help a CEO to perform more effectively. Instantly, she said 'yes'. And before she told me what it was, she added:

'It's one of the most important things for *anyone* – in any walk of life, in any role – if they want to grow as a person. If they want to become more effective, and to understand themselves better.'

'Well,' I said eagerly, 'what is it?'

'Discover what is in your blind self' she replied.

For me, this was an extraordinary statement. Not because I hadn't any idea what she was talking about – I knew *exactly* what she meant by 'blind self' – but because it was the first time since my stroke that I'd heard those exact words.

In fact, it was around eight years previously that I'd first learned about this concept. I'd been introduced to it by a mentor as a young CEO, when I'd been very keen to try and understand how to make myself more successful and effective. By working with this mentor, and understanding how my 'blind self' was holding me and the company back, I was able to become far better at my job.

Nearly a decade later, there I was on a golf course, talking with a business psychologist about a concept that I realized could be a fundamental building block for changing course. I don't know who was more surprised: me for hearing about the blind self again so long after I'd first encountered it, or Helen for having a caddie who knew exactly what it was.

Your four 'rooms'

So, what is the 'blind self'? Well, as you may know, it's part of a leadership and management tool developed by the author and philosopher Charles Handy. He called the tool the 'Johari House' and its aim is to develop self-awareness (based on an original idea by Joseph Luft and Harry Ingham in 1955).

Handy believed that in order to do this, you need to be aware not only of how *you* see yourself, but also of how *others* see you. Sometimes, what you see in yourself is what others also see, but at other times you'll have a view about yourself that others don't see at all.

The Johari House is Handy's analogy for a person, and the concept can be applied to you, to me, or anyone.

Within the Johari House there are four rooms:

- Room 1 is the part of you that both you and others see – *the public you.* For example, you may be incredibly well organized. You focus on timelines and deadlines, you set up routines and you are disciplined. You know that, and everyone around you knows it, too.

- Room 2 is the room that contains the aspects of you that *only others see*; you yourself are not aware of them – this is *the blind you.*

- In Room 3 is the subconscious part of you, which is seen neither by you nor by others – *the unknown you.* This is the part that traditional psychologists like to talk about: Freud's area!

- Room 4 is your private space, the part *you* know but keep from others – *the hidden you.* This is the room where you keep your most intimate thoughts – the things you would not tell anyone else about.

For me, Room 2 is the most fascinating of the rooms in the Johari House. Here are some examples of what is meant by it:

You may believe that you are a good chair of meetings, but in fact, if you talked frankly with the people who attend the meetings you chair, they'd tell you that they are unfocused, run late and often move off the agenda.

Or, when you attend your daughter's sports day, you are 'competitive mum', but don't realize it. You believe that everyone thinks the way you do about these things. However, if you had a chat with a number of your friends, they'd tell you that you are the *most* competitive person they know. You want to win at *everything* – and that includes your child winning the egg and spoon race!

Your blind self contains aspects of your behaviour and personality that can either hold you back, or propel you forwards to make a success of changing course.

Make room 2 smaller

When I found out about the idea of the blind self, my mentor suggested I ask my leadership team to compile two lists: one noting all the things I did that were effective and helpful, the other highlighting aspects of my behaviour that were annoying, unhelpful and stressful. To my surprise, both lists were extensive, but the 'annoying and stressful' list was much longer than the first list.

I was aware of some of the things on that second list, but a number of them were completely new to me. One prominent item centred on pitching for new business, which was a key aspect of my role and a very important part of the company's work. The process was stressful for all those involved in preparing the documentation, developing the presentations and attending the pitch meetings.

As CEO, I'd decided that I would take on the role of coordinating the whole pitching process. In addition, I wanted to bring a calm and relaxed atmosphere to it. I honestly believed I was good at both of those things, but my team thought otherwise. They told me I would get very wound up and anxious, and that therefore I wasn't calming the situation at all. I was also poor at coordination – often asking for things at the last moment and frequently failing to communicate regularly with the team.

Part of my blind self had certainly been revealed!

After this painful feedback, I decided that someone else – someone more relaxed, more focused and more organized – should lead the pitch team. I would be involved mainly at the very beginning of the process, and at the very end. Strangely enough, the company very quickly became more successful at winning pitches.

So, if you're going to thrive on this journey of changing course, you'll need to become much more aware of *your* blind self. There may be aspects of your behaviour or your personality that are holding you back, or on which you should focus more time.

You'll need to discover better and more efficient ways of doing things. One of the main ways of achieving this is to make your blind self *smaller.* There are two aspects of your blind self that you need to focus on, and the first is this:

Become much more aware of the things you think you're good at but actually aren't.

For example, because pitching was such a key and important part of leading Company Net, I wanted to be in charge of the whole process. But the strengths required to coordinate and organize this process – focus, discipline and communication – are not my key strengths. In fact, I'm very weak in those areas.

However, I still tried to make myself believe that I *was* good at them. I tried to use strengths I didn't really possess. To everyone else this was plainly the case, but not to me. If I'd been more honest with myself, listened to my leadership team and become more aware of aspects of my blind self, I'm certain I would have been better at my job.

So, I suggest that you make a list of the things you *believe* are your strengths; the things you *think* you're naturally good at. Then ask trusted family and friends if they agree with what you've selected. If there are strengths on that list that *you* think you have, but which your family and friends *don't*, you must listen to them! Use this insight to find ways of managing your limitations.

The second aspect to focus on is this:

Consider whether there are parts of your blind self that you could be using more of to help you when changing course. Do you have strengths that you're ignoring, or are unaware of? Are there things you're naturally good at, but aren't doing?

It was only after the stroke – when I had the time to really talk to my friends and family, and my neuropsychologist, on a regular basis about my future – that I started to become aware that I'd been ignoring some of my strengths. Ironically, I found I could use these strengths to help me as I was changing course.

For example, everyone told me – separately – that they felt I had a great talent for being adaptable when situations changed or new opportunities presented themselves. And things changed constantly after the stroke!

And when I really thought about it, and was honest with myself, they were right – I actually did (and still do) thrive on change. I like it when new things happen. I enjoy having to react to new situations. In the past, I'd resist too much change – I thought I needed to be focused and disciplined – but by becoming aware that I'm good at being adaptable, I have worked out that it is better for me to do a number of smaller roles every day rather than one main one.

Recognizing and acting on that ability to adapt made my change from a CEO to a caddie (and all the other roles I now do) much easier and more successful. With the help of my family and friends, I was able to make my blind self a bit smaller.

So, ask the people you really trust in your life to list the things *they* think you're really good at. Look to see if there are things common to these lists. Are there things on them that surprise you? Are there strengths there that you have but which you aren't using, for whatever reason? Remember Chapter 3: Be Like Detroit? If the answer is 'yes', changing course could give you the opportunity to start using them properly.

Listen to those people you trust in your life, as they'll help you to reveal, explore and understand your blind self. They can see aspects of your behaviour and personality that you can't – both good and bad! Act on what they say. Then focus on what you're really good at, and manage those areas where you have limitations.

Make your blind self smaller and, as Helen said, it could be one of the most important things you do to help make your changing course journey a success.

Chapter 16

PURE INSPIRATION

Identify role models

Many of the people I caddie for are entrepreneurs – people who've taken the risk of setting up their own business and have made a success of it.

Sarah from Boston was an entrepreneur – and a very successful one at that. I could really relate to her world because she was an internet entrepreneur, as I had been before my stroke. That aside, she was just a really nice person to spend time with.

Sarah had built up her internet business in the 1990s, had grown it rapidly in the early 2000s and then sold it for a serious amount of money in 2004. Since then, she'd invested in a number of other software and technology companies and had made even more money.

As we walked up the 5th fairway, Sarah asked me about my background. I told her that I too had set up and run an internet company in the 1990s and 2000s. She seemed genuinely interested and was fascinated by my story.

For the next few holes we shared stories of our experiences as CEOs. We both agreed that, even though the role was incredibly fulfilling, it did have many challenges. As we chatted, I asked Sarah if there was one thing, more than any other, that helped her do the job (as I have done with other people). Immediately, she said: 'role models'.

'Throughout my life, I've always had role models', she explained. 'People I can look up to – to inspire me and motivate me. Some of these people I knew well – an old boss or a favourite teacher, for example. Others I never met, but I read books and watched TV programmes about them. Wherever possible, I even went to conferences to listen to them talk.'

Bill Gates had been one of Sarah's role models when she set up her company. Although she hadn't met him, she was genuinely inspired by what he'd done with Microsoft – how it all started, how he got his first clients, and how he grew the business from just him and Paul Allan to one that employed thousands of people.

What Sarah said about role models had a huge effect on me. For the rest of the round, when I wasn't talking to her or trying to find her ball (she wasn't a great golfer!), I was thinking about what she'd said. And the more I thought about it, the more I realized how important it is to have role models when your life is going in a new direction.

Who inspires you?

In the years immediately following my stroke, there were a number of people whose lives and stories I found incredibly helpful and inspiring. Looking back, I can see they were my role models. As Sarah discovered, these were the people who really motivated and encouraged me and, by using them as an example, I was able to see what might be possible for me.

One of these role models was a lady called Dr Jill Bolte Taylor, whose story had a huge effect on me. She'd written a book called *My Stroke of Insight* about her stroke and how she'd recovered from it. A friend suggested I read it, and after doing so, and watching Dr Taylor speak at a conference in 2008 (via a website called TED), I began to believe that one day it might just be possible for me to do something like she'd done. As a role model, she gave me a target to aim for and showed what might be possible for me.

So, from my own experience, I know that it's hugely beneficial to have role models when it comes to changing course. In fact, I think they're *essential*, especially if you're doing something new or different, so I advise you to identify some.

Your role models might be people you know, or people you've never met, but what they will give you is a sense of direction on your new journey. It's best to have more than one role model, as you can take the parts of these people's lives that inspire you and apply them to your own situation.

Try to learn from your role models: aim to follow their example. They will provide you with inspiration – whether through their achievements, their characters or their wisdom.

I'm often asked how I coped with having to give up my job following my stroke. Until I caddied for Sarah I would say things like, 'I've always been a positive person so I just had to accept it and move on', or 'I've always had an entrepreneurial mindset, and starting again is something I like doing.'

Even though these statements are true, I also turned to a number of role models who really helped me as I changed course. As well as Dr Taylor, there was the journalist and author Fergal Keane, whose memoir *All of These People* inspired me to change my lifestyle after my stroke.

Then there was the passion that two close friends had for the African country of Rwanda, which gave me the idea to use my business skills and experience in a completely different context.

I also admired Steve Jobs for the way he started again after Apple sacked him in the 1980s. He showed me that it's possible to be successful second time around. Then there was the author and web development entrepreneur Jason Fried, who'd been successful both as a business person and as an author. And that's what I was hoping to achieve.

From these role models I was able to get the inspiration and motivation I needed to do the new things I'm now doing in my life. They have shown me that:

- I can write a book and get it published.
- I can be actively involved again in the business I co-founded 16 years ago.
- I can use my previous business experience to help other companies grow and be successful.
- I can jointly set up and help run a social enterprise, The Together Partnership, which works with companies and individuals in Rwanda in Africa and Scotland.
- I can have a more healthy and balanced lifestyle.

Now, I don't list these things as a way of saying, 'Look at me, aren't I great?' Rather, it's to show the importance of role models. In the immediate months after the stroke, I wouldn't have believed that *any* of the things I've listed above would be possible. But, because others – those who became my role models – had done similar things, I wanted to follow their example.

Who would you invite to dinner?

So, try to identify role models you can look up to. Take the specifics of what they have achieved and apply them to your own changing course journey. This will be invaluable. However, it may not be immediately apparent exactly *who* your role models are, as you may not have thought of anyone in this context before. So here's an idea of how to go about it.

Imagine that you're going to invite some people over for dinner to celebrate the fact that you've changed course. You can only invite five guests and they must be people you find inspiring and motivating – either because you admire one of their character traits, because they've achieved what you are about to attempt, or because you are in awe of what they do, or have done, in their lives.

So, *who* would you invite? They can be historical people or living ones. They can be someone from your family, or a business person who lives thousands of miles away. Whoever they are, let's agree that these are your role models.

So the next time you're questioning what you are doing on your new journey, or when an obstacle seems to be in your path, or simply when you need some motivation, have a look at your dinner invitations – *those* are the people who'll give you the inspiration you need to achieve your plans, goals or dreams. You'll discover that they'll help you enormously.

There's something else you'll need when changing course, and that's lots of practical help, advice, suggestions and support. But where can you find this? Well, caddying for Mike showed me how powerful your existing network of contacts can actually be.

Chapter 17

ONLY FOUR FROM BARACK OBAMA

Understand the power of networking

Have you heard of the theory of 'six degrees of separation'? This contends that, because we're all linked by chains of acquaintance, we are just six introductions away from any other person on the planet. In other words, you are linked by a string of six or fewer acquaintances to the Queen, the Dalai Lama and the President of the USA – in fact, anyone in the world!

In the late noughties, software giant Microsoft conducted research to see if this theory could be backed up in reality, and, amazingly, they found that it could. After studying billions of e-mails and electronic messages, the company proved that any two strangers are, on average, distanced by precisely 6.6 degrees of separation.

Since then, both Facebook and Twitter have proved that two people anywhere in the world are distanced by less than five degrees of separation.

Caddying for Mike from Washington, DC demonstrated to me that the people from Microsoft, Facebook and Twitter are right. In fact, there are only four degrees of separation between me and Barack Obama. Here's how.

Mike was a retired lawyer, and he was playing golf in Scotland with seven of his friends. They were a nice group to be around and very relaxed. They'd been in Scotland for a week and this was their last round before flying home the next day.

It turned out, though, that there were only six other golfers left on the trip: one of their party had been called back to the USA the day before. As I chatted to Mike on our way round the course, he told me that this person was the brother of a former president of the USA.

Now, this former president of the USA has met Barack Obama many times, and knows him well. So, there you have it. Because I caddied for Mike, I am only four introductions away from the current president of the USA: me to Mike, to the brother of the former president of the USA, to the former president of the USA, to Barack Obama!

It's all about connections

You're probably thinking that this is all very interesting but what on earth does it have to do with changing course. Well, quite a lot really, and here's why:

If you understand the power of connections, and utilize the networks you currently have, or which are available to you, the chances of you making a real success of changing course will be significantly increased.

I strongly suggest that, if you don't already have one, you develop a positive attitude to the concept of *networking*. By this, I don't mean just the *business* concept of networking, I mean *all* of your networks – personal, social and business. This is because, regardless of what you're planning to do, you're going to need a great deal of help, support and advice along the way.

'Just do something that you'll love doing and everything will turn out fine' won't work on its own. You see, the challenge starts with the 'do' word, and you've probably recognized that there are three potential obstacles with that, namely:

- You don't know exactly what that 'something' is.
- You know what it is, but you don't know how to achieve it.

- You know what it is, but current circumstances (probably financial) mean that you have to do something else.

Understanding the power of the connections you already have, and utilizing those connections, could be vital in helping you to overcome any of these three obstacles.

Just to be clear, a connection, or a network, is *anyone* you have a link with. It might be a relative, a close friend, a former colleague, the woman who runs the coffee shop where you buy your espresso, the man you talk to on the beach when you're walking your dog. It's someone that you have a relationship with – however tenuous.

Today, with social media sites like Facebook, Twitter and LinkedIn, you don't even need to physically see these people. You'll have connections right around the world, and your network is constantly growing. Take some time to think about how big your potential network *could* be, and how many potential connections you have. You may well be surprised!

To illustrate this point, let me tell you about my own experience with LinkedIn. I currently have just over 350 direct connections – friends, former work colleagues, people I've had a business relationship with, people I've played golf with and so on.

But, if I look at *their* connections – just one degree of separation from me – that number increases to well over 70,000 (assuming that each of my 350 connections has, on average, about 200 contacts of their own). That's my potential network, and even a small percentage of that number could be a fantastic resource for help and advice.

Just ask

I make this point not because I intend to contact all these people, but to highlight the fact that *your* potential network is much bigger than you probably realize. You don't need a website like LinkedIn or Facebook to show you that – just go to your address book, your mobile phone contacts, your Christmas card list, and recognize that for each person you know on that list, there will be tens or hundreds of *their* contacts who could potentially help you as you change course.

The key to unlocking potential help and advice is simple: just ask for it. Your contacts can help you overcome some of the obstacles that are stopping you from moving forwards on your new journey. They can help you to move faster, and more effectively.

For some of you, asking for help will be difficult. You might be a reserved kind of person, or you might be embarrassed about what's happened to you. Or you might be someone who has never used their network to develop a new career or tackle something completely different.

Perhaps the idea of contacting someone you don't really know makes you very nervous, and that's understandable. But there's a great way of countering those thoughts and that's to imagine that the shoe is on the other foot.

Would *you* mind if someone you knew, or someone who was referred to you by a friend, called or e-mailed you for your advice or help? I'm pretty certain that you'd try to help, and indeed that you'd be pleased to be asked. And if you couldn't help, the likelihood is that you would recommend someone who could.

So, that's all you'll be doing – asking people for help, advice or suggestions – and 'just asking' people within your network is one of the most important steps you can take, because it can significantly help you make a success of changing course.

On my changing course journey, what has amazed me is that, regardless of whether it's been my wife, a close friend or someone I hardly ever see, people have invariably been willing and happy to help me. I just needed to *ask*, and if they couldn't help me directly they very often knew someone who could.

I found that, as long as people didn't feel they were being exploited or taken for granted, they were delighted to help and give me their time; they were happy to point me in the right direction, or introduce me to someone else they felt could help me.

A colleague and friend said this to me when I told him of an idea I'd had about setting up a social enterprise: 'I would love to help, but I don't know how. You tell me more about your idea and what you're looking for, and I'm sure I can give you some suggestions or put you in touch with someone who can help you.' And he did help me – all because I just asked him.

This conversation was invaluable because, with the help of others, I then went on to co-found a social enterprise which forges connections between business people in Rwanda in Africa and Scotland – The Together Partnership.

Writing this book is something else I wouldn't have thought was possible after the stroke, but it *has* happened, in part, because I asked some of my connections if they'd help me to achieve it. They were delighted to do so, and this book is proof that utilizing your networks really can work.

So, whatever your dream – opening a restaurant, going back to university, travelling the world, taking a career break, setting up a business from home now that your children have left, applying for that new job – just start *asking* people in your network if they can help you to achieve it. It's very likely that they'll have the contacts in their own network that could make all the difference.

Although I caddied for Mike, I don't think I'll try to contact Barack Obama just yet. But you never know. One day I might just get in touch!

You'll know *who* to contact, and *when*, if you just trust in your instinct. Let me introduce you to Jane, who highlighted the importance of going with your gut feeling.

Chapter 18

30 SECONDS

Trust in your gut feeling

I don't know whether Jane from London had read British-Canadian author and journalist Malcolm Gladwell's book *Blink,* but they shared a strong belief in the power of intuition – making decisions based on your gut feeling.

Gladwell's book is about those moments when we *know* something without knowing why. In it, he explores the phenomenon of 'blink', which shows how a snap judgement can be far more effective than a cautious decision.

Jane certainly used the 'blink' idea in her job as a headhunter in the City of London, and to great effect. She'd travelled to Scotland to interview a potential candidate, and had decided to turn her visit into a long weekend – and to include a game of golf with her husband.

During the game, I asked Jane if there was any set method for 'headhunting'. She told me that, for her, there wasn't – it was more dependent on the *type* of role she was headhunting for. She also made a comment that I found fascinating, and with which, I think, Malcolm Gladwell would agree.

Jane explained that she'd been doing this type of job – recruitment and headhunting – for 15 years, and that she knew within about 30 seconds of meeting a candidate whether or not she'd employ them for her clients.

'I just go with my gut feeling,' she said.

'But what about formal interviews and psychometric tests?' I asked.

'Well, they're all useful, and I do use them, but I've found over the years that trusting in my gut feeling with candidates has served me well. The majority of the time, I really *do* know within a very quick timescale if the person I'm meeting will be suitable for a particular job.

'Yes, I'll do background checks on them – references, CV checks and so on – but as long as they all stack up, my gut feeling is usually right. Then I get people I really trust to challenge me on the decision I've made to see if it holds good. And you know, nine times out of ten, it does.'

So, Jane was trusting in her gut feeling and then putting some checks in place to confirm it. As Gladwell says in his book, 'Truly successful decision-making relies on a balance between deliberate and instinctive thinking.' It seemed to me that Jane had got this balance right in her job as a headhunter.

As you change course, you'll need to trust in your instincts even more than usual. Some people call this 'going with your gut feeling'; others call it a 'hunch' or a 'flash of insight'. Whatever you call it, see it for what it is – a very powerful tool. Trust in your gut feeling and listen to what it's telling you about any situation you are in.

When you're making life-changing decisions that may make you feel overwhelmed, you really need to trust in what's already present and available within you: your own natural homing device, your internal GPS system – your intuition. It's usually right.

Go with your gut feeling on anything: ideas, insights, things you want to do, proposals you're presented with. Then talk to someone you trust to see if it stacks up. Make your checks, talk to the 'experts' to see if your initial view was correct, but always believe as a starting point that your gut feeling will be correct. You'll really be surprised by how many times this turns out to be the case.

Follow your heart and intuition

But don't just take my word for it. In the USA, the New Jersey Institute of Technology studied the relationship between intuition and business success. They found that 80 per cent of the executives whose company's profits had more than doubled in the past five years had above-average precognitive powers. Essentially, these people were trusting their instincts with the big decisions they had to make.

In addition, a management professor at the University of Texas found that, of the 2,000 managers he tested for intuition, the higher-level ones had the top scores. This demonstrates a definite link between the use of intuition and career progression.

Even some of the most *logical* thinkers of all time made their greatest discoveries based on flashes of intuition. Think of Sir Isaac Newton and the apple that fell on his head, or the ancient Greek mathematician Archimedes shouting 'Eureka!' in his bathtub. And here's what Einstein said: 'The only really valuable thing is intuition.'

In *Blink,* Gladwell cites numerous examples of the power of intuition. The first of those happens in the opening pages, when he tells a story about an ancient Greek statue that the Getty Museum in the USA was considering purchasing. The museum did all the usual background checks to help establish authenticity, and after 14 months of research and investigation, the staff finally concluded that the statue was genuine and purchased it.

However, when an art historian saw the statue, he declared it a fake in an instant. Another art historian then took a look and he too felt and sensed that the work wasn't right somehow. A third expert claimed to feel a wave of intuitive repulsion.

So, further investigations were carried out, and these led to the discovery that forgers in Rome had sculpted the statue. The teams of analysts who did the 14 months of research turned out to be wrong, and the historians who relied on their initial hunches and intuition were right!

As a CEO, I relied strongly on my intuition, and more times than not I was proven right in the decisions and the actions I made. For example, I decided to call a potential client for no reason other than that I had a *feeling* I should call. I sensed there might be a business opportunity for us.

Perhaps I'd read something in a newspaper, or maybe it was a conversation I'd had with a member of staff. Whatever prompted me to do it, I just felt I should call the client. And strangely enough, there *was* an opportunity!

Then there were occasions when I decided to send more information to a client than was required. This was based on a mere *feeling* that they'd find it useful. It was, and it helped to cement our relationship further.

Often, my decision to employ certain staff was based on the fact that I trusted them as soon as they walked into the room at the interview. These people turned out to be our best and most loyal employees.

Conversely, when I've *not* gone on my intuition – when it was screaming one thing but I ignored it and listened to others who convinced me to change my view – that, in the main, is when I've made bad decisions. For example, there was the case of the potential investors who wanted to invest in Company Net. When I first met them I had a gut feeling of distrust. However, I was persuaded that they'd be good investors.

To cut a long story short, my gut feeling was proved right, and these investors turned out not to be as good as everyone believed. What they'd told us about themselves proved, in some aspects, to be completely false.

Then there was the person I was persuaded to employ, even though I'd had a bad feeling about him at his interview. Once he was working for us, he turned out to be one of our most difficult employees.

The decisions I made by not listening to my gut feeling cost us dearly – both financially and emotionally. Steve Jobs famously said, 'Don't let the noise of others' opinions drown out your own inner voice. And most important, have the courage to follow your heart and intuition.' I wholeheartedly agree.

Listen

Since I was forced to change course, I've relied on my intuition far more than I've ever done in my life. I've had to do this, since I no longer have a large team working for me. And you know, I think I've become better at making decisions. Maybe it's because I don't have a lot of people questioning or challenging my decisions that I find it easier to make them.

Or perhaps – as I've been 'just doing it' – I've had to make decisions more quickly and be more responsive to new ideas and opportunities that'll help me. Again, maybe it's because I'm trying to spend more of my time doing things that involve my talents that I find listening and acting on my intuition easier.

Whatever it is, I've found that I've relied on my gut feeling much more, and the more I do that, the more I seem to move forwards positively in my new life.

In the initial stages of changing course, you'll probably have a lot of quiet time – or you might often be on your own. One of the things you can do during this period is listen to your intuition:

Think about the decisions you have to make, or the many ideas that are flying around in your mind. Take some time out to walk, run, cycle or meditate – anything that will allow you to listen to what your gut feeling is telling you – and then listen to the first answer that pops into your mind.

This isn't easy, because several thoughts might flood into your mind. But try to remember the one that came first. *That is your intuition at work.* If you want reassurance, chat to someone about the answer or decision that your intuition is giving you. I'm confident that this'll be the right decision for you.

Jane found that by using her intuition she was making the right decisions most of the time. So, as you change course, just trust your gut feeling – it could be invaluable.

Chapter 19

ZEN AND THE ARCHITECT

Practise mindfulness

Have you seen the film *Meet The Fockers*? It's a comedy starring Robert De Niro, Ben Stiller, Dustin Hoffman and Barbra Streisand, and is a sequel to *Meet the Parents*. In one of the opening scenes, we're introduced to the 'Fockers': Dad Bernard (Dustin Hoffman), who's a hippie and a retired lawyer, and mum Roz (Barbra Streisand), who's a sex therapist. The pair come across as people who have an alternative lifestyle, one aspect of which is Zen Buddhism.

My perception of Western practitioners of Zen Buddhism was of people like the Fockers – people who are a bit wacky, a bit alternative, and perhaps from California!

Claire was professional, mainstream and 'normal'. She lived in San Francisco, California, and was an architect with her own thriving practice. And she was also an avid practitioner of Zen Buddhism and its philosophy.

This became apparent through her attitude on the golf course. After every shot, good or bad, she'd have the same reaction: acceptance. If she hit a great shot she was happy. If she hit a bad shot – well, she was still happy. Actually, happy is the wrong word. She seemed relaxed. Determined to do well on every shot, but (and this is the key) she would *accept* the outcome, whatever it was.

This doesn't mean that Claire was a laid-back hippie. She wanted (and was determined) to play well. No, it was the *attitude* she maintained throughout the game – regardless of how well she played – that made an impression on me.

After eight holes of witnessing this, I commented that most people I caddie for don't react like her. Many become angry with themselves if they hit a bad shot, I explained. Others give the impression of mentally giving up after a number of bad shots, while others forget that they're on holiday and meant to be enjoying the golf.

Claire laughed at this and said, 'Well, they should practise mindfulness.'

Mindfulness, she went on to explain, is a key part of Buddhist philosophy, and it's something she'd been doing for 20 years. She strongly believed that it's relevant to everyone in the modern world – a very simple concept that means paying attention in a particular way, 'on purpose, in the present moment and non-judgementally'.

The key word here is 'present'. Achieving this, Claire said, helps to increase awareness, clarity and acceptance of our current situation, whatever that may be – from hitting a golf ball to attending a meeting or cooking a meal. Mindfulness trains us to accept the moment as objectively as possible.

Put simply, mindfulness is noticing thoughts, physical sensations, sights, sounds, smells – anything we might not normally pick up on – but doing it in the present moment. It's choosing and learning to control our focus of attention. And, when the moment has passed, to then let it go.

By doing this, Claire explained, you accept the present moment as it is. Your stress levels fall, your mind rests and you start to learn to accept things the way they are. However, she said, although the actual skills might be simple, because it's so different from how our minds usually work, it takes a lot of practice.

The here and now

To me, it sounded fascinating and incredibly helpful. You see, when I caddied for Claire it was only 18 months after my stroke, and at that time, there was still much uncertainty surrounding my future. Some of this was real, but I also had worries and anxieties that were not based on any facts (remember Chapter 12: Predictive Texting). Either way, my mind was going into overdrive because for me, as with many people, uncertainty is very stressful.

I was desperate for something to help calm me down and remove some of the perceived uncertainty. For a while, I'd taken medication for this, but I'm a strong believer that drugs only give you respite – they don't tackle the real issues. So, after three months, I stopped.

Then I met Claire, and learned about her belief in the value of practising mindfulness. After I caddied for her that day, I went back to my computer and searched for 'mindfulness'. There was a huge amount of information on it.

I bought a number of books on the subject, and talked to a psychologist friend who said that mindfulness is now seen and accepted as 'mainstream'. The more I learned about it, the more I realized how much it could help me. Eventually I started to practise mindfulness – and the effects were incredibly beneficial.

One of the main ways I do that is through meditation – mindfulness meditation. If you'd told me years ago, while I was still heading up Company Net, that I'd be practising mindfulness and meditation, I'd have laughed. I'd have dismissed it as the preserve of Tibetan monks – something I didn't have time for.

But since caddying for Claire, I understand how mindfulness and meditation can help anyone. The effects are amazing, and once you understand how to do it, just 15 minutes a day can make a real difference to your life.

Mindfulness enables you to relax. It helps you to think more clearly about things. It also seems to rest the brain – to stop the constant 'chatter' that goes on in your head. Essentially, it teaches you how to accept the things you can't control and control the things you can.

Since I started practising mindfulness, I've been able to concentrate on the 'here and now'. I've become more aware of how issues of the present affect me, and I either do something about them, or I just acknowledge them and let them pass me by.

And consequently, I've become less stressed because I feel more in control.

Put the glass down

As I've said before, changing course can be a very uncertain time. Your mind might be moving at 100 miles per hour. *Everything* may seem urgent. You might feel depressed or anxious. You'll probably feel that you aren't in control of your circumstances, struggle to make decisions and feel very stressed. Or, all of the above!

I recently came across the following story, which highlights perfectly how important it is to be aware of your stresses and to let them go:

A psychologist is teaching stress management to an audience. She raises a glass of water and everyone expects to be asked the usual 'glass half empty' or 'glass half full' question. Instead, with a smile on her face, she enquires: 'How heavy is this glass of water?'

The audience calls out answers ranging from 240ml (8oz) to 568ml (20oz).

The psychologist replies: 'The absolute weight of the glass doesn't matter. It depends on how long I hold it for. If I hold it for a minute, it's not a problem. If I hold it for an hour, I'll have an ache in my arm. If I hold it for a day, my arm will feel numb and paralysed. In each case, the weight of the glass doesn't change, but the longer I hold it, the heavier it becomes.'

She then elaborated on this: 'The stresses and worries of life are like that glass of water. Think about them for a while and nothing happens.

'Think about them a bit longer and they begin to hurt. And if you think about them all day long, you will feel paralysed – incapable of doing anything.

'It's important to remember to let go of your stresses. As early in the evening as you can, put all your burdens down. Don't carry them through the evening and into the night. Remember to put the glass down!'

In my experience, mindfulness and meditation can help you to put the glass down. I can assure you that if you get into practising mindfulness regularly, your new journey will be more successful, less stressful and more enjoyable. You will feel far more in control of all aspects of your life.

As I've discovered, there are so many resources, both on- and offline, that can teach you all about mindfulness and meditation. I enrolled on a practical course, led by an 'expert', that taught me some simple techniques and exercises that I could use daily.

I still use them today, whenever I feel stressed or anxious about a situation. And it works every time.

I would recommend that you try to inject some mindfulness into your daily life as you change course, either by reading a good book on the subject, or by joining a class. Whichever route you take, do try it out, as it will bring you a sense of peace, calmness, self-acceptance and self-control.

Be like Claire, and try to live in the moment as much as you can. And while you do this, take the time to notice all those people in your life who are helping you change course. Meet Jake, and the small gesture that he made which had a big effect on me.

Chapter 20

THE WALLET

Appreciate everyone

Moments before the start of the 200 metres final at the 2012 London Olympics, the Jamaican sprinter Usain Bolt noticed that a volunteer kit girl was looking nervous. He asked her why. 'I'm so excited,' she said.

'What she said was really funny,' Bolt said afterwards, 'but that's the thing I like to do. I like to talk to them, smile at them. I always bump fists with the person who is carrying my bag, just to show appreciation.'

I'm pretty certain that Usain Bolt hasn't met Jake from Philadelphia, but they have a very similar philosophy on how you should treat people – whoever they are.

As we walked down to the 16th hole, Jake said to me: 'Can you stop, please? I need to get something out of my bag.' I put the golf bag down and Jake opened the side pocket and took out his wallet. He then took out some money and proceeded to walk towards the greenkeepers, who were standing on the side of the fairway allowing us to play the hole.

I watched and listened as Jake gave £30 to the head greenkeeper and said: 'Buy the guys a few beers on me tonight. The course is in brilliant condition. Thanks for all the work you do to keep it that way.'

I watched the reaction of the head greenkeeper. First, he tried to refuse the money, but Jake was insistent. He then took the money, and with a huge smile he and the other two greenkeepers who were with him shook Jake's hand.

Jake then walked back to me and asked: 'Is it a 5 iron or a 6 iron to the pin?'

I've caddied for hundreds of people and I'd never seen anyone do that before. I told Jake that what he'd done was a great gesture. 'I just wanted to thank them,' he said. 'They are the people that we don't really see, but they make our lives much easier and more enjoyable.'

Jake was the CEO of a very successful real estate company with hundreds of employees. Why did he tip the greenkeepers? It wasn't to impress his friends – they were further up the fairway, and so didn't see him do it. Nor did he do it to impress me. He asked me to wait as he went off to talk to the greenkeepers – I had no idea what he was doing.

No, like Usain Bolt, Jake just wanted to show his appreciation for other people. And I think that's fantastic. Don't you think that the world would be a better place if there were more people like Jake who – whatever they do or earn – take the time to appreciate the things that others do for them?

I do, and caddying for Jake started to make me realize how much support, encouragement and help I'd had since my stroke. Up to that point, I suspect I'd taken nearly everything that was given to me for granted. There were many people – and there still are – who just wanted to help me. There was nothing in it for them as I was back at the beginning – my status and my old title gone.

Take time to say 'thank you'

Believe it or not, that little gesture of Jake's really did help me to start appreciating the way Company Net supported me after my stroke; the love and care I've had from my family; the medical professionals who went that 'extra mile'; the encouragement and help from friends and colleagues; the offers of new types of work that would help me recover and open up opportunities for me.

All of these things have made my changing course journey a success, and many people have helped make my life far easier than it might have been.

It's such an important part of the changing course journey to keep appreciating everyone, and everything they do to help you. Continue to show your appreciation – and let people know that you're grateful for their support.

There is a danger that if you *don't* actively show your appreciation, people may just stop helping you. Life will start to become far more difficult as a result, and this might derail your new journey.

I'm embarrassed to say that this happened to me shortly after I'd had my stroke. There were people who gave me huge emotional support in those early stages but, because I didn't show how much I appreciated them, or more importantly, they didn't *feel* appreciated or valued by me, they moved on and are no longer a big part of my life.

Even though my change of direction has gone well, I'm certain that things might have been better if I'd shown more appreciation to those people. I definitely took them for granted and I am a lesser man because of it.

It's all too easy – as I found – to become so immersed in your changing course journey that you simply *forget* to say thank you. Don't make the same mistakes as I did: it will only make things more difficult than they should be.

If you don't already have one, foster an attitude showing appreciation to all the people who are helping you. By doing this, you are offering the gift of feeling valued, and great things start to happen to all involved.

As long as you show genuine appreciation to the people who are helping you, they begin to feel more valued themselves. And that can only benefit their lives.

A very close friend of mine, who is one of the people to whom I should have shown more appreciation over the years, has a wonderful philosophy to life. It's summed up in a statement that he uses to sign off his e-mails:

> *'When you are at your best, you do great things, you think great thoughts and you feel great. That's because you are receiving and giving the experience of being valued.'*

I can't be certain whether Usain Bolt or Jake from Philadelphia feel valued themselves, but the way they act shows me that they *do* believe in the power of making other people feel valued by showing them appreciation. As you change course, I'd advise you to do the same. It will make things a lot easier for you, and give the people who help you a real sense of being valued.

When you start to *really* appreciate what your family, friends and co-workers do for you as you change course, you start to realize what a brilliant opportunity this gives you to sort out what your priorities will be as you go forwards. And Gary from Vancouver understood exactly what the *number one priority* should be.

PART 5

CHANGING COURSE LIFESTYLE

Chapter 21

THE DOCTOR'S FINAL CHANCE

Don't forget the world of your family

Sometimes when you read an article in a newspaper, or find a story on a website, you aren't sure whether it's true or just an urban myth. That was my dilemma when I read about Sam Walton. One of the most famous entrepreneurs in the world, Walton took a small general store and grew it into one of the largest global corporations – Walmart. Apparently, though, on his deathbed his last words were: 'I blew it.'

During his lifetime, Walton was regularly referred to as the richest man in the world. He worked hard to grow his empire, and had all the trappings of a very successful lifestyle. But, in the last moments of his life, it seemed that he realized there were other, more important, things than money, business and success – things like friends and family. Hence his final words.

Regardless of whether or not this story is true, I believe it provides a great insight into one of the potential benefits of changing course. You now have the opportunity to look at your priorities in life and work out which are the really important things, before it's too late.

Gary from Vancouver reinforced this point when I caddied for him. He was playing golf in Scotland with his son, Jack. Gary was a cardiologist, and Jack had just finished college and was about to start working for an investment bank in New York. Age-wise they were mid-late 50s and late 20s respectively. Both were excellent golfers and great to caddie for because they were so friendly.

As we chatted, I discovered that this was the first time they'd been on a golfing trip together. Previously, Gary had gone with colleagues, or as a guest of a pharmaceutical company, while Jack had gone on trips with his friends.

It was Gary who told me that the main focus of this trip was to spend time together, just father and son, and play some of the greatest golf courses in the world. He said that Jack had been on at him for years about doing a trip to Scotland but he'd just never got around to arranging it.

He'd always been incredibly busy with work commitments – research papers to write, conferences to speak at and so on. Next year we'll do it, he'd always promise. But next year was as busy as the year just gone, and so they'd never got around to making the trip. Until now!

It was Jack who'd finally 'persuaded' his father to take the trip. He was due to start working for the bank in the autumn, and he knew that he'd have less time for holidays in the future. This was probably their final opportunity to holiday and play golf together.

So, finally, here they were playing golf in Scotland on a beautiful summer's day, with me as their caddie. Gary summed it up: 'It is one of the best things I've done, coming on this trip. There will always be work opportunities, and things to be done, but playing golf with my son in Scotland and just spending time together is an experience I would not have missed for the world.'

Sort out your priorities

One significant benefit of changing course is that it gives you the opportunity to sort out your priorities. It allows you to work out the right balance for the time you spend on all areas of your life – your work, your family, your friends and yourself. In my experience, and obviously in Sam Walton's too, family is often the first thing to be sacrificed when we think there are more important and urgent things to be done – most often work and business commitments.

However, as Gary realized, you can't get back the 'lost time' that you didn't spend with your family. Changing course allows you to put this right as you go forwards in your new roles – and it'll be one of the most important and life-changing strategies you make.

My role as a CEO consumed *everything* – my time with friends, my desire to exercise regularly, and crucially, my time with my family. I believed, both consciously and unconsciously, that work was the most important thing in life.

I'd read the books that contained the same message that this chapter communicates – spend quality time with your family – but my thinking went something like this:

> *Yes, that's fine, but spending time with my family won't win us new business or sort out the cash flow problems. I'm doing this now so I can spend more time with my family in the future. I have a business to run. My staff and my clients really need me. The company will probably fail without me as the CEO. My family is managing fine without me.*

So, I jumped on planes to see clients, I went to conferences, dinners and events, I worked late into the evening at the office and brought work home with me. While that was happening, there was another world I'd dive into for an hour or so – sometimes longer on the weekends (if I was not away) – and that was the world of my family.

This was a world in which my children were growing up, where stories were shared, where events that happened at school were discussed, where meal-time arguments and discussions took place, where parents' evenings were attended, and where rugby, football and hockey games were won and lost.

And in the main, it was a world I wasn't really a part of – I had a business to run.

Then I had the stroke. And my belief that work was the most important thing in my life was kicked right out of the window. The world of my family, which I'd dipped into all too infrequently, turned out to be way more important than running a company.

Changing course because of the stroke forced me to alter the balance of the priorities in my life. It made me understand that the time I'd *not* spent with my family was lost time. I came to the conclusion that I would never make that mistake again.

The stroke forced me to understand that Company Net *could* survive, indeed thrive, without me. My clients talked to other people in the company. Staff dealt with my e-mails and phone calls. The meetings with potential clients still happened. A new CEO took over. As I write this chapter, the company is flourishing, with a great CEO, a fantastic leadership team and a wide range of new and long-standing clients.

I came to understand that some of the things I thought were important were not so crucial after all. I *was* replaceable. The company went forwards without me. I found out that, while it's still important to have business or personal success, family time must not be sacrificed to achieve it. There's a world inhabited by your family, and I found I needed and wanted to play more of a part in it.

Find the right balance

I discovered that the small things – like meeting my son at the school gates and chatting with him as we walked home, watching my daughter play hockey, and going for a coffee with my wife during the week – are far more rewarding than board meetings and long plane journeys.

It was changing course that gave me this insight, and made it possible for me to spend far more time with my family. This is one of the best things to come out of my adventure so far.

As Stephen Covey says in his excellent book, *The 7 Habits of Highly Effective People:* 'Most of us spend too much time on what is urgent and not enough time on what is important.'

Take the time to really examine what's important to you. Start off on your new journey determined to find a balance in all areas of your life. I believe that whatever you define as your family should be in the 'top priority' column of your life.

Get involved in the world of your family: it's the place where you'll find out what's really important. You'll discover, I'm sure, that if you get the balance right between your family world and everything outside of it, it will provide a great platform from which to try new things in your life.

Definitely do the things which you love doing, but make sure that you don't sacrifice your family time to do it. Because if you want to do things that you feel make a difference in your own life, you'll naturally want to spend time with your family and make a difference to them, too.

It's there that you'll find a real, genuine feeling of value and purpose, and that's the essence of the feeling you get when you are making a difference in your life.

Whatever you do when you change course, don't do it thinking that, if you work really hard, one day you'll be able to spend quality time with your family. It will never happen. Remember the story of the Mexican fisherman in Chapter 10?

Turn that idea upside down and think: *I want to spend quality time with my family now, and changing course has provided me with the opportunity to build a better balance in my life. I'm not willing to sacrifice that principle.*

You won't regret this decision, and neither will your family. This is one of the greatest benefits of changing course. And, as Gary found out, you'll discover the real meaning of success – being able to spend more time with the people who mean most to you.

There's another principle based around your friends that you shouldn't compromise on. Stefan knew this, and he had a great view on it.

Chapter 22

WHISKY AND VENISON

Don't neglect your friends

On occasion, I caddie for someone who has a philosophy that is so obvious and simple but so profound that I think, why don't more people take it on?

Stefan, from Hamburg in Germany, was near the end of his round when he made a remark that I thought was just great. For the whole game, he'd been very relaxed and really happy to be playing. He was a good golfer but he made mistakes and went into the rough more than once. However, he never got angry or frustrated.

When I asked him why he was playing golf in Scotland, he told me that this trip was a twice-yearly event, and that he'd been doing a similar one with the same group of friends for many years. Sometimes it was Scotland, other times Ireland, and on a few occasions they'd played in the USA. As we were walking up the 18th fairway, I commented that he seemed to be a very relaxed person.

Stefan look surprised: 'How on earth could I get stressed playing golf here in Scotland?' he asked. 'I'm so happy just being here, playing golf with my friends, drinking lots of whisky and eating wonderful Scottish food, especially venison. I have enough stress in my job back in Germany. I'm just delighted to be here.'

His is a philosophy I love. It seems a fantastic one to have – not only about playing golf, but also, more importantly, about the benefits of friendship.

Stefan was a finance director for a large multinational company, and because he was spending time in Scotland with his friends he was happy, relaxed and stress free. He was definitely out of 'work mode' and into the friendship one when I caddied for him, and it was obvious that his friends were very important to him – twice a year, without fail, he would go away with the same group.

Friendship matters

This practice of spending regular time with friends is a crucial one when you're changing course. As I highlighted in the last chapter, spending more time with your family is one of the great benefits that can come out of this process, and I believe you should apply a similar philosophy to spending time with your friends. Don't forget about them as you forge your new path.

However, it's all too easy to do just that when you are immersing yourself in something new. You'll feel consumed by unexpected events and situations. But, as I mentioned earlier, you also go through a whole range of emotions and experiences – some stressful, others exciting, boring, challenging or exhilarating. So, to help you through those, or perhaps just to share them with you, you'll need the emotional and social support that comes from spending time with your friends.

It's difficult to define *exactly* what friendship is, but I like this attempt by the great boxer Muhammad Ali:

> *'Friendship is the hardest thing in the world to explain. It's not something you learn in school. But if you haven't learned the meaning of friendship, you really haven't learned anything.'*

After my stroke, the friendship of others was paramount as I came to terms with my situation and started to undertake a number of new roles and activities. I discovered how friendship manifests itself in different ways: there's the friendship of help, support and advice; the friendship of relaxing, laughing and just taking my mind off other things; the friendship of someone just being there to talk to; and the friendship that helped to motivate me. Without my friends, I wouldn't have been able to make a successful transition onto a new path in my life.

When you are changing course, there won't be one friend who can do everything for you – you'll need a number of them, each of whom will provide you with different things, depending on their strengths and on how they fit into your life.

Coincidentally, I talked to one of my friends about this, and he pointed me towards a book that backs up my own experience.

The roles and strengths of your friends

Vital Friends, by Tom Rath, builds on the idea that we all have strengths as people in general, but also as friends. These manifest themselves in the different types of roles we take on in our friendship with each other.

In reading the book, I've found that my friends' strengths, and the roles they take on, actually *complement* my limitations. Some friends are good at motivating, others are good at listening and giving me their wisdom, while others have challenged me with new ways of thinking and doing things.

According to Tom, there are eight vital roles that close friends might play in any given situation or event. Some play only one role; a few play several; none play *all*.

Here's a brief summary of the roles that Tom believes friends can offer:

Builder

Builders are great motivators, always pushing you towards the finishing line.

Champion

Champions stand up for you and what you believe in.

Companion

A Companion is always there for you, whatever the circumstances.

Connector

Connectors are bridge-builders who help you to achieve what you want, then connect you to others.

Collaborator

This is a friend with similar interests to you own: someone you can easily relate to.

Energizer

These are your fun friends, the ones who always give you a boost.

Mind opener

Mind openers are the friends who expand your horizons with new ideas, opportunities, cultures and people.

Navigator

The friends who give you advice and guidance, and keep you headed in the right direction.

When I went through these categories, I could see all my friends' strengths, and the roles they have played for me. I could identify many examples of when, as my friends, they'd used their strengths for my benefit, especially as I changed course.

This might sound a bit clinical, but I do think it's very important to understand and accept that your friends provide you with different things. Most of the time we aren't aware of the particular roles we're adopting as friends for each other. The trick, though, is to recognize that friends will give you different types of help and support. Don't neglect any of them, as they can *all* help you, in their own different ways, to make your new life a success. And your friendship with them will become even closer, which can only benefit all concerned.

In my old life, I'd become so immersed in my work that spending time with friends became a rare thing. I might see them on a Saturday night, once a month, say, but meeting them regularly for a coffee or a beer midweek was unusual. And, perhaps unsurprisingly, this seemed to be the situation many of my friends found themselves in – like me, they were just too busy doing work things.

It was only when I had to change course that I really started to appreciate the value of proper friendship, and how certain friends were really helping and supporting me.

In the last chapter I talked about getting a balance in your life. Changing course allows you to do that, but it's also an opportunity to go on a new path, a different direction, in your life. You'll be at a crossroads, and there might be a number of options for you.

At this time, then, I would recommend that you stay close to your friends. They will help you to make the right decisions and choices at that crossroads, and support you on your new path. Like your family, they'll be invaluable and will help you to examine what your real priorities in life should be. You'll also learn more of what true friendship is.

Make a conscious effort to see your friends regularly, but appreciate that, unlike you, they probably won't be in the middle of changing direction in their lives and may well be consumed by their current challenges, roles and work. So, meet them when and where it's most convenient for them. Understand, too, that they'll all bring different strengths and take on a variety of roles for you, as you do for them.

As long as they feel they are not being taken for granted, or exploited, your friends will love helping and supporting you. And that in turn will strengthen your relationship. This is just one of the many life-changing benefits of changing course.

Another is that the process provides you with a reason to change some areas of your lifestyle that may be harmful. In other words, to break bad habits.

Chapter 23

CHANGING HISTORY

Break bad habits

When I look back on the caddie jobs I've done, I realize that some strange coincidences have occurred. Very often, something has been going on in my life about which I'm undecided, or uncertain how to proceed. It might be a business idea, a health worry, or just some general situation that's bothering me.

And then I caddie for someone who helps me, or in some way guides me, often without even realizing it, to the best course of action, because they have experience in the very problem I'm struggling with. One of these coincidence occurred when I caddied for John from Washington.

John was in Scotland with some friends from his golf club. He was a really nice guy, but not very talkative, so I just left him to himself. Around the 8th hole he asked my advice on choosing a restaurant for that evening. I recommended a couple of local places, and told him that, in addition to the great food they serve, both have an excellent selection of malt whiskies.

He told me that the latter would be wasted on him as he was a non-drinker, but that his friends would make up for him. I laughed and commented that only the day before, my wife and I had been discussing *my* drinking habits.

John was keen to chat more about this, so I told him I was certain that I was drinking way too much, especially for someone who'd had a stroke. Even though my stroke hadn't been brought on by my lifestyle, I wanted to reduce the chances of having another one. Also, I was keen to lose some weight.

However, I was worried that I'd miss out on things if I stopped drinking alcohol. It had been such a big part of my life – dinners, beers with clients, corporate entertainment, drinks after caddying, a large whisky (or two!) after a hard day.

So, I was still having a debate with myself about whether I should stop drinking altogether or just drastically reduce the amount I drank instead.

John then volunteered that for many years he'd had a serious drinking problem: in fact, he was an alcoholic. He'd drink every day, and his relationships with his wife, his children and his friends suffered badly because of it. However, with the help of Alcoholics Anonymous, and the support of his family, he had decided to stop.

That was 12 years previously, and he'd not had a drink since. As a result, his relationships, and his life in general, were much, much better for it. What was ironic about this was the fact that he worked in a winery!

John told me that giving up alcohol was the best decision he'd ever made. Then he looked directly at me and said: 'From what you've told me about your drinking habits, I would strongly suggest that you think about stopping drinking alcohol for at least six months. You'll not regret it.' I like the direct approach you get from a lot of Americans – they just say it as they see it!

That round of golf with John helped me to stop drinking completely for well over a year. And he was right – I didn't regret that decision. In fact, I believe it was one of the best decisions I've made since changing course. I'm pretty certain that if I hadn't had the stroke, I'd still be drinking at levels way beyond the recommended weekly limit. And I realize now that wouldn't have been good for my health or my relationships.

Changing course gave me the wake-up call I needed to change what I saw as one of my bad habits. I thought to myself: *why don't I take this opportunity to try to change course in some other areas of my life I'm pretty sure are doing me harm, health-wise*. This allowed me to draw a line in the sand about my drinking.

A great excuse to start again

Changing course can give you the impetus to review your lifestyle and change it for the better. It can give you a *reason* to do this. If you've decided to try something new in your life, you could also take this opportunity to look at the habits and behaviour that might be causing you harm – smoking, drinking too much, being overweight, not exercising – and do something about them.

In *All of These People*, Fergal Keane repeats a great line he heard his counsellor use: 'The history can stop here and now. It can be a different history.' This philosophy inspired him to stop drinking.

Changing course gives you the chance to write a *different* history for yourself. I know from personal experience how difficult it is to deal with harmful habits, and I'd never presume to give advice and guidance about this. There are fantastic organizations that provide specific support – you can search for these online – or you can talk to your friends or utilize your network. You'll be amazed how much help is out there.

However, what I've found is that changing course almost inevitably brings a new and different mindset – one that's about starting again.

The idea and concept of 'starting again' is a powerful one. When you want to try to break a habit, or adopt a new one, the idea that you can start again – have another go – is a great way to help you change your thinking.

I once had a client who was a marketing director of a large organization. Over the years that Company Net worked for him, I got to know him well and we'd meet for lunch or have a beer on a regular basis. On one of these occasions, he told me that he was about to resign from his job because he no longer liked what he was doing for a living.

He explained that he hated the 'politics' at work, and was being asked to do things that he felt uncomfortable with. Also, on a personal level, he was concerned about being overweight, and the fact that he didn't have time to exercise as his job consumed all of his time. His plan was to leave and set up his own consultancy.

I saw him again about 18 months later – after I'd had the stroke – for lunch. By then, he was running his own small consultancy and was loving it. He looked great and had also lost a lot of weight. He told me the latter was down to some advice about getting fit he'd received from an old friend: 'Now that you are running your own consultancy, make sure that you put four weekly appointments with the gym into your diary. Treat these as your most important client – a meeting you *cannot* cancel.'

Changing course can be the catalyst for creating a new mindset that will allow you to rethink your habits and lifestyle, as it did for my client. It enables you to shape your thinking along these lines:

> *Right, I now have the impetus and motivation to change the negative habits that were embedded in my old lifestyle. I have a reason to do things differently now – a reason to break negative habits and create positive new ones. I can start again.*
>
> *I've no history or experience against which to gauge my performance in this new environment: I'm like a 'fresher' at university, at the beginning of a new phase of my life. And this new situation will be marked by my desire and willingness to break a bad habit.*

For me, changing course was an opportunity to make new commitments to myself. Some of those were related to what I'd do with my time, and what my priorities would be. I also made one about my lifestyle: to stop drinking alcohol for at least six months. That commitment was successful, and I put this down to the new attitude that came with changing course and the concept of starting again, as well as the support of family and friends.

It also came from the time I spent with John as his caddie, and the example and encouragement he gave me on how he had turned things around. A good role model!

As you embark on a new part of your life, take this opportunity to really examine your lifestyle. You might find that you're completely happy with it and don't need to make any changes. If so, that's terrific. However, if you have a gut feeling there's an area that you really should sort out, then grab the chance to do something about it. Adopt a new attitude to help you make the changes that will significantly benefit you.

There's another, similar attitude, and that's the idea that you have a reason to challenge some of your old thinking. You can apply this not only to your main role in life, but to all the others, too. To show you what I mean, let's meet Scott.

Chapter 24

A DAY HAS 24 HOURS, NOT 7.5

Look at all your roles

I would have been envious of Scott from New York if he hadn't been such a friendly person to caddie for. Instead, I just admired him. Whatever or whoever determines what we'll be good at in life certainly went into overdrive with him!

Not only was he a surgeon at one of the city's top hospitals, he was also a scratch golfer – his handicap was 0. (For non-golfers, that simply means he was an excellent player.) I've caddied for hundreds of people now, and I can count on one hand how many of those were scratch golfers. Physically, Scott seemed very fit – he told me that he ran most mornings before breakfast.

On top of all this, he was on the board of one of New York's leading art organizations, and that was why he was in

Scotland. He was combining his golf trip with his board role by attending a number of events at the Edinburgh International Festival. Still only in his early forties, he was married, and had two young children who'd come with him on the trip. Jealous? Me? Not at all!

But how did he fit it all in – the career, the golf, the family commitments, the regular exercise, the board duties?

'I just love doing all these things, and I make sure I commit enough time to all the different roles I take on,' Scott explained. 'I've learned to manage my time effectively, and I don't really watch television. A day is 24 hours long, not the 7.5 hours that most people think it is. I also have great support from my family.'

Scott's remark about a day being 24 hours long is an important idea to embrace as you change course. I believe that most people think they have only one main role in life – as a parent, director, entrepreneur, student and so on. This is how we identify ourselves. And when we want to change direction, it is usually this main role that we are thinking about changing.

Changing course not only gives you the chance to take on new roles, it also allows you to examine the roles you already have. You can look at your life as a whole.

To be clear, a role is not just a person's occupation. It can be anything, from being a husband, a runner, a stamp collector, a musician and so on. Your roles are how you spend your time, every hour of the day.

We move seamlessly from one role to another throughout the day, sometimes consciously, at other times unconsciously. As you know, we usually define people by what they do for a living, but this 'occupation' or 'main role' usually takes up only about a third of a working day. A further third is generally spent sleeping. But what about the remaining hours in the day?

If you think about it, there's no reason why you can't apply this book's philosophy, ideas and insights about changing course to your wider, *non-occupational* roles. So, let's take a look at these. Do *they* make you jump out of bed with excitement? Do they make you feel that you're making a difference? Are there any other roles – outside your 'main' one – that you'd love to be doing?

A different kind of working week

As a CEO, I bought into the theory that the only way to be successful was to work 60 hours a week on my 'main' role. I read interviews with entrepreneurs in which they'd talk about their normal working week, and it seemed that they all did roughly the same thing. They'd plan their coming week on Sunday evening, be sat at their desks no later than 8 a.m., then work until 6 p.m. or 7 p.m. (at least) every weekday and some of the weekend, too.

Each day would be packed with meetings, lunches and networking events. They all had one main role (their occupation) and that took up most of their time. I was like that, too, and I believed there was no other way to do it.

But, a funny thing happened when I was forced to change course. Once I could no longer do my old role – and had recovered as much as I could from the effects of the stroke – I suddenly had all this free time. Yes, I really needed to earn money, but I was partly restricted in what I could do.

The idea of running a company again was out, mostly because parts of my brain were not working properly. But working full time, for five days a week, would also now be too much for me to cope with.

So I had to learn how to work smarter, and to manage my time far more effectively. I accepted that I couldn't have one main role again, and started to look for a *number* of roles that I could do during a normal day. This turned out to be one of the best things to come out of changing course. It showed me how to do work differently, more effectively, and far more enjoyably.

Today, I do this by focusing on a role for a maximum of 2–3 hours at a time. Then I focus on another role. My working day doesn't stop at 6 p.m. I dip in and out of my various roles every day. An hour doing one role, then an hour doing another: I have no fixed working hours.

Sometimes I start early in the day; other times I work late into the night. Some roles bring me an income; others don't. Some I've had for a while, from before the stroke; many are new. So, over time, and by really focusing on my strengths, by using my network, by trusting my instincts and by believing that I *could* do new things, I was able to build up a number of roles and then undertake them in a way that would minimize the effects of the stroke.

If you asked me today what my role or occupation is, I'd say that I have a number of them: a dad, a husband, a caddie, an author, a non-executive director, a director of a social enterprise, a consultant and a friend. All of these are roles, and I'm passionate about all of them.

I think I achieve far more now, during a normal day, than I used to. I no longer see myself as having a working week – I just organize my roles based on when I can do them most effectively for all concerned.

Do all your roles excite you?

Now, I completely accept that what I do wouldn't suit everyone, but the point here is that changing course should be a life-changing process that you apply to *all* areas of your life. You can do the things you are passionate about for 24 hours a day (well, outside of sleeping!), not just 7.5 hours.

Changing course gives you a reason to look closely at how you spend your time. If you plan to change your main occupation or role, and tackle something that you'd love to do, then why not take that approach with everything else that you do?

For example, if, for you, changing course means leaving your job and setting up your own business, why not also take up painting, if that's what you've always wanted to do? Or, if you've decided to enrol on a college course now that the children have left home, why not also start to write that book you've always felt was a great idea? If your job has been made redundant and you've decided to volunteer at the charity you so admire, why not – seeing as you've always had a passion for technology – also learn how to build websites?

See if you can find a buzz of excitement, and a real sense of purpose, in the things you do other than your main role. If there are challenges you'd like to take on, now is the perfect opportunity.

See if you can find a smarter and more effective way to carry out your main role that will allow you to dip in and out of the other roles you love to do and are passionate about.

In *The 4-Hour Work Week*, Timothy Ferriss says: 'The question you should be asking isn't "What do I want?" or "What are my goals?" but "What would excite me?"'

'What would excite me?' is a great test question for the things you do in your waking hours. It doesn't mean that every moment will be rosy, easy or particularly challenging, but what it does mean is that the roles you do (or the ones you'd like to be doing), should, in the main, give you a feeling of excitement and purpose. You should be looking forward to the time when you'll be doing them.

If all your roles give you those feelings then, like Scott, you'll find that a day is much longer than 7.5 hours, and that you really will have changed course in all areas of your life.

So, we're almost at the end of the book, and there's no better way for me to finish up than to introduce you to Rob.

Chapter 25

COMING HOME

Getting your purpose back

In my years as a caddie in Scotland, I've noticed that playing golf here has a magical effect on some people. They feel honoured to playing in the 'home of golf'. They are fascinated by the game's history, and they love playing the challenging links golf courses. They are also impressed by everything Scotland has to offer, including its beautiful scenery, local food and drink, and warm hospitality.

Rob from Melbourne epitomized this category of golfer. He was playing golf with his wife and six of his friends, and this was their last round before flying home. The group had a late afternoon tee-off time on a lovely Scottish summer's day. One of the joys of a Scottish summer are the long light evenings – visitors love it, and Rob was no exception. As we walked up the 18th fairway the sun was just starting to dip.

Halfway down the fairway Rob stopped and looked back across the golf course, to the harbour and the sea in the distance. 'This whole trip has been fantastic,' he declared. 'It has exceeded my expectations in all areas. In a way, I feel as though *I've come home*.'

For some golfers, then, it just feels natural to be here – like 'coming home'. Most have planned and thought about the trip for years beforehand, and when they finally arrive, the experience is everything they'd hoped for and more.

If you do it right, changing course can give you a similar feeling of 'coming home' – the sense that what you are doing has a purpose, and that it brings you contentment. It just feels natural and right.

Hopefully, this book is giving you ideas, insights and suggestions to get you excited and inspired about changing course. You can use these to rediscover your purpose, to do the things and perform the roles where you are using your strengths for most of the time and feel that you are making a difference.

A look in the mirror

Changing course can give you the reason and the inspiration to start again in all aspects of your life, or to fix something that isn't really working. So embrace it. As you go forwards, it can give you a second chance to get the priorities right in your life.

There's a story I love, told to me by a very good friend, which describes this so well.

A philosophy professor stands in front of his class. Wordlessly, he picks up a very large, empty glass jar and proceeds to fill it with golf balls. He then asks his students whether the jar is full. They agree that it is.

The professor then picks up a box of pebbles and pours these into the jar, too. He shakes the jar lightly and the pebbles fall into the spaces between the golf balls. He asks the students again if the jar is full, and they agree that it is.

Next, the professor picks up a box containing sand and pours this into the jar. Of course, the sand fills up the remaining gaps. He asks once more if the jar is full and the students respond with a unanimous 'yes'.

The professor then produces two bottles of beer from under the table and pours their entire contents into the jar, effectively filling the tiny spaces between the grains of sand. The students laugh.

'Now,' the professor says, as the laughter subsides, 'I want you to recognize that this jar represents your life. The golf balls are the important things – your family, your health, your friends and your favourite passions – and if everything else was lost and only they remained, your life would still be full.

'The pebbles are the other things that matter, like perhaps your job and your house. The sand is everything else – the small stuff.

'If you put the sand into the jar first,' he continues, 'there's no room for the pebbles or the golf balls. The same goes for life. If you spend all your time and energy on the small stuff, you'll never have room for the things that are important to you. Pay attention to the things that are critical to your happiness.

'Spend time with your children. Spend time with your parents. Visit your grandparents. Take your spouse out to dinner. Play another 18 holes of golf. There will always be time to clean the house and mow the lawn.

'Take care of the golf balls first – the things that really matter. Set your priorities. The rest is just sand.'

One of the students raises her hand and enquires what the beer represents. The professor smiles and says, 'I'm glad you asked. The beer shows you that, no matter how full your life may seem, there's always room for a couple of beers with a friend.'

I think this sums up perfectly the changing course philosophy: identify the golf balls first, and then the pebbles in your life, and spend most of your time on those things – not on the sand. Pay attention to the things that are critical to your happiness.

Consider the messages in this book in relation to all the roles you occupy. If these roles don't make you happy, excited or contented, it probably means you need to change course.

If my wife or one of my friends had told me seven years ago that I'd soon resign from the company I'd co-founded and become a caddie, I'd have thought they were insane. At that time, I believed my life was great – which, in the main, it was. I thought my future was pretty much planned out, and that I'd be doing my job for a long while to come.

But now my life has changed completely. With the help, guidance and support of so many people – together with the brilliant opportunity that caddying gave me to meet such fascinating and inspiring golfers – I'm doing things and occupying roles I never thought would be feasible or practical.

I had to change course from being a CEO, yet I've found a number of other roles that give me the same feeling of purpose that once gave me. Caddying, and the people I've met through it, have taught me so many new things and have brought me insights into what's really important in my life.

I don't pretend that I have all the answers, or that I do all the right things. Nor do I feel happy and contented every hour of every day. Far from it. But I believe that, in the main, changing course has allowed me to spend my time doing things I love, because I have applied the philosophy, principles and mindset outlined in this book.

In sharing some of my own stories, experiences and insights with you, I hope that I've given you the inspiration to change course so that you, too, will jump out of bed every morning because you love what you do.

I included some words of wisdom from Steve Jobs in my first chapter, and I feel it would be fitting to close with another quote from him: one that sums up everything I've been trying to convey in this book. He said this when he gave the Stanford University commencement speech in 2005:

> *'I have looked in the mirror every morning and asked myself: "If today were the last day of my life, would I want to do what I am about to do today?" And whenever the answer has been "no" for too many days in a row, I know I need to change something.'*

Changing course – and doing it with the help of this book – means that when you look in the mirror every morning and ask yourself the question Steve did, your response should be a huge, loud and resounding 'yes'!

How great would that be?

Conclusion

THE 19TH HOLE

Your changing course journey

One of the great joys of playing golf is arriving at the 19th hole. This is a term used by golfers and non-golfers alike to describe the clubhouse. The North Berwick Golf Club clubhouse is the ideal 19th hole: it's located in a beautiful old building, with fantastic views over the golf course to the beach and the sea beyond. It also serves a wide range of drinks, and good locally sourced food.

As a caddie, I've been invited countless times to join the golfers in the clubhouse after their game. For me, it's great to just sit and listen to them talking and laughing – reviewing their round and discussing the individual holes. For the golfers themselves, it's a time to reflect on what happened during the game, and what didn't (a putt that should have gone in...), and the new experiences they have gained.

As I reflect, '19th hole' style, I think it would be helpful to provide an at-a-glance round-up of the key themes of *Changing Course.* You can dip into this part of the book whenever you need a reminder of these, or are looking for help, support, advice or tips for staying on track.

Part 1: Changing Course Foundation

Aim to make the following very straightforward principles the basis of everything you do on your journey:

- **Love what you do.** Only take on roles or jobs that you feel passionate about – ones which excite you and make you want to jump out of bed in the morning.
- **Have a sense of purpose, of meaning**. Aim to feel that you are making a difference in what you do, and in the roles you take on.
- **Use your innate talents (or strengths) for most of the time**. Because when you do, everything you undertake will feel easier and more natural.

Part 2: Changing Course Mindset

While the principles above are the foundation for changing course, your mindset is the *framework* that will support your progress along the way. Develop an attitude that will enable you to do the following:

- **Believe** that what you are planning to do will be a success. The belief you have about something will create the momentum for you to keep going.

- **Take intelligent risks**. Don't take daft ones. Understand the difference between the two and always take the intelligent risk.

- **Be yourself, and stick to your own principles**. Don't follow the crowd, and remember that it's okay to be you and to follow your own dream.

- **Look forwards, not backwards**. Embrace the new opportunities that are out there for you. View the things that have happened in the past as an opportunity to learn, rather than with regret.

- **Focus your energy on the 'pull and push reasons'** for wanting to change course, and stop looking for excuses not to do it. There are *always* ways of getting around the obstacles in your path.

- **Just *do* it**, rather than just *thinking* about doing it. Don't let your circumstances, or what people might think about you, determine your decisions. Always remember that the decisions you make today shape the 'you' of tomorrow.

Part 3: Changing Course Traps

Make sure you're aware of the various traps that can send you off course. Try to stick to the five 'personal commitments', as they can help you avoid these traps. So, whatever you are planning to do as you change course, remember the following:

- **Don't follow the money**. Try not to look at a job's salary before you have successfully applied the three principles of changing course in Foundation.
- **Keep your feet on the ground**. Don't do things just because they look or sound great on TV, in the movies or in a book – stick to *your* reality.
- **Look only at the *facts***. In any given situation, avoid making assumptions or predictions based on half-truths and little hard evidence. Don't let your mind run wild with 'what if' scenarios.
- **Accept whatever situation you find yourself in**. Don't spend your time wondering what might have been, or wishing you could turn the clock back.
- **Accept that you have limitations**. Develop strategies to manage them so you can spend most of your time focusing on your strengths.

Part 4: Changing Course Discoveries

Uncovering new aspects of yourself, and doing things in a different way, are two of the most exciting and motivating outcomes of changing course. To achieve the maximum benefit, though, you'll need to:

- **Understand your blind self** – the part of you which *you* don't see, but which everyone else *does*. Be willing to change, or develop further, the aspects of your blind self that you uncover.
- **Identify your role models** – the people who really inspire and motivate you. Ensure that you have more than one, and refer back to what you admire about them and their character to help you stick to your chosen course.
- **Foster a new attitude to networking**. Be aware that your potential network is probably much bigger than you realize. Don't be embarrassed to ask for help.
- **Let your intuition guide you** on the decisions you have to make. Don't dismiss your gut feeling – listen to what it's saying to you.
- **Practise mindfulness and meditation**. Wherever possible, live in the 'now'. The benefits of doing this will be calmness, acceptance and self-control.

- **Don't take anyone for granted**. Value all the people you come into contact with. Show your appreciation to everyone who is helping you to change course.

Part 5: Changing Course Lifestyle

Finally, and crucially, take the opportunity that changing course gives you to look at *all* aspects of your lifestyle, and do the following:

- **Ensure that your family is the top priority in your life**. Allow enough time for them. Remember that you can't get lost time back, and you cannot 'bank' it now to use in the future. Make sure that family time is the most important entry in your diary.
- **Make time to see your friends regularly**. Don't hesitate to ask them for their help, support and guidance. Have a good understanding of what their strengths are, but don't take them for granted.
- **Break bad habits**. Ask yourself if there are habits and practices in your lifestyle that may be causing you harm. Take the opportunity that changing course offers to break some of them by 'starting again'.

- **Apply the foundation and mindset for changing course to *all* the roles you fulfil**. Remember, a role isn't just your main occupation – it's the things that you do in all areas of your life. Look at the roles that really excite you and try to spend most of your time doing them.

- **Identify the golf balls, the pebbles and the sand in your life**. Focus most of your time on the golf balls, and then the pebbles.

- **Ensure** that most of what you do is what you would want to be doing if this was your last day on Earth.

Finally, I hope that all the inspiration, ideas and insights in this book have given you food for thought, and that changing course will be as exciting and life-changing for you as it has been for me.

CREDITS

Handbook for The Soul, Richard Carlson, 1996, Sheree Bykofsky Associates. Reprinted by permission of Benjamin Shield and the estate of Richard Carlson.

The 4-Hour Work Week: Escape the 9-5, Live Anywhere and Join the New Rich, Timothy Ferriss, 2009, Vermilion. Reprinted by permission of The Random House Group Limited.

No Limits – The Will To Succeed, Michael Phelps, 2009, Simon and Schuster.

The Truth About You: Your Secret to Success, Marcus Buckingham, 2008, Thomas Nelson.

The 7 Habits of Highly Effective People: Powerful Lessons in Personal Change, Stephen Covey, 1989, Free Press.

Blink: The Power of Thinking without Thinking, Malcolm Gladwell, 2007, Back Bay Books.

Rework, Jason Fried and David Heinemeir Hansson, 2010, Crown Business.

NOTES

NOTES

NOTES

ABOUT THE AUTHOR

Neil Francis has numerous years of experience as a CEO, non-executive director and director. He is also a caddie at the North Berwick Golf Club in Scotland.

In 1996 he co-founded, then led as CEO for 11 years, one of the first internet and web development companies in the UK – Company Net. During his time as CEO, he worked with some of the biggest international brands – Disney, Coca-Cola, BP and Microsoft – on projects around the world. He led the team that sold Company Net and then two years later led the team that helped to buy Company Net back.

He is currently a director of two software companies. He is also co-founder and director of a social enterprise, The Together Partnership, which creates partnerships between Scottish and Rwandan individuals and companies. In addition, he founded and runs a consultancy – the CEO to Caddie Consultancy – which works with companies, CEOs and senior leaders to help them embrace and implement new digital, software and technology strategies.

Neil and his family live in North Berwick, a beautiful seaside town south of Edinburgh. A typical day for Neil might now include a board meeting in the morning and caddying in the afternoon.

www.ceotocaddie.com